The Seven Apocalyptic Seals

from

Rudolf Steiner

Adrian Anderson Ph.D.

Threshold Publishing, 2020
www.rudolfsteinerstudies.com

Distributed by Ebook Alchemy
Prahran, VIC
Australia 3181

ISBN 978-0-6481358-8-3 (hbk)

ISBN 978-0-6481358-9-0 (paperbk)

Contents

Illustrations

Every true spiritual image, such as those in the Book of Revelation or in these seven seals, which are related to those in the Book of Revelation, has a mighty effect on the human being, stimulating impulses in the soul.

Rudolf Steiner (lect. 28th Nov. 1907, GA 56

It makes a great deal of difference whether the air around the Earth is filled with spiritual thoughts or thoughts concerning material things.

Rudolf Steiner (lect.19th May 1909), GA 104a

Photograph of the Conference participants, giving a glimpse of the seals placed around the hall, and the two columns.
Next to Rudolf Steiner is Marie Steiner, second on her right is Anne Besant.

Introduction

Coinciding with the festival of Pentecost in May 1907, at the 4-day annual International Conference of the Theosophical Society in Munich, the seven "Apocalyptic Seals" were displayed. As Rudolf Steiner was General Secretary of the German Branch of the Theosophical Society at that time, the arrangements of the Conference became his responsibility. This enabled him to bring the artistic element into Theosophical meetings; an idea which was developed further after his closest student and friend, Marie von Sivers, requested that this be undertaken. Consequently, the program included classical musical and vocal performances, recitation of poems by Goethe, and the performance of a play by Eduard Schuré.

The hall was also decorated with esoteric artistic images, including these seven 'apocalyptic seals'. These were painted by Clara Rettich, based on sketches provided to her by Rudolf Steiner. These original large paintings were not preserved. The images in this book are copied from the images made available in 1977, by the Rudolf Steiner Archives in their invaluable folio, *Bilder Okkulter Siegel und Säule.* They were reproduced from the second set of the seals, made in 1911, also by Ms. Rettich.

Concerning the artist and her work

Unfortunately, there is an astonishing lack of records about the artist and the process whereby she created such superbly painted images. I cannot even honour her by giving the date of her birth and death, or any comments from Rudolf Steiner. All of this is unknown, and could not be traced. The request in 1911 for the second set of the seals was made specifically by Rudolf Steiner, for use in the Stuttgart Anthroposophical Centre. This tells us of his positive response to her work. Although the Stuttgart building was destroyed in the 1930's, this second group of seals survived, and are in the care of the Rudolf Steiner Archives Administration in Dornach.

Sources of Rudolf Steiner's explanations of the Seals:

These are mainly published in volume 284/5 in the Complete Works, *Rudolf Steiner: Bilder okkulter Siegel und Säulen.* (Published in English as *Rosicrucianism Renewed.*)

1: **Lecture 21st May, 1907**: given at the International Theosophical Conference held in Munich when the seals were displayed.

Note: this 'lecture' was not a formal session of the Conference; it was actually held discreetly before a small group of participants. As the Conference Program Guide for the 21st May reveals, this lecture is not listed on that page, so it was not formally part of the Conference (see Appendix). Although these seven extraordinary images are the most striking and significant esoteric images displayed in the Conference hall, it appears Rudolf Steiner considered that they were to be too esoterically powerful to be the subject of a keynote lecture.

We can conclude that his explanation of the seals on the afternoon of the 21st May, was intended primarily, but not exclusively, for those Theosophists who were members of an un-orthodox Freemasonry Order, known as the Rites of Memphis and Mizraim. This Order was highly respected by those Theosophists who were interested in Freemasonry, and they had asked Rudolf Steiner, in 1904, to lead their lodge meetings. Rudolf Steiner edited the texts of this Order, giving them an esoteric orientation more compatible with his own esoteric wisdom. This activity was in effect a branch of the Esoteric School within the Theosophical Movement. Rudolf Steiner was one of the

Leaders of this School for Theosophists in Europe. The sessions of the School, and of the informal Masonic group, were held only for those Theosophists who were invited to join; members did not publicise nor refer to, their closed meetings to Theosophists in general. It appears that this is the reason that the talk about the seals on this day was given without any fanfare. (See the Commentary on Seal Four, for more about this Freemason aspect.)

However, after the Conference, it seems that much interest in the seals was aroused amongst those Theosophists who respected Rudolf Steiner's works, and consequently he gave a formal lecture about the seals to Theosophists in Stuttgart. He also briefly wrote about them in his written Report for the journal of the Theosophical Society. In addition, he arranged for a small folio to be produced in October of 1907, of reproductions of the seals, in black and white. For this folio he wrote a brief Introduction, explaining what the seals portrayed.

2: **Rudolf Steiner's Report** on this Conference, written in the summer of 1907.

3: **A lecture on 16th Sept. 1907**, about the seals, given in Stuttgart (also in GA 101).

4: **The folio brief description** he wrote in October 1907, when the Seals were published in small black/white format.

In the days prior to the Conference, Rudolf Steiner delivered a number of lectures on the subject of The Book of Revelation in general to Theosophists in Munich; this would have greatly assisted the audience to understand the brief explanations of the seals given at the Conference. But to clarify the perspectives given in regard to the seals, for this book, I have also drawn on my study of all of his 53 lectures on the general subject of the Book of Revelation.

Minor References

A: at the end of a lecture from 19th Oct. 1907, in Berlin (in GA 284/5)
(A brief note about the need to avoid displaying them in everyday areas)

B: In a lecture from 28th Nov. 1907 (in GA 56)
(Some brief words about Seal One)

Note:
The Book of The Revelation of St. John, the last book in the Bible, presents a dramatic but also veiled narrative of the spiritual battles and triumphs that humanity is to undergo on its journey into near and distant future Ages. Powerful graphic descriptions of our future and the spiritual powers engaged in this dramatic journey abound in its pages. Hereafter I shall refer to this book simply as, Revelation. This book is also often referred to as 'the Apocalypse', which is taken from ancient Greek title of this book.

Why are they called Seals, where do they come from ?
Rudolf Steiner did not give any specific answer to these questions. But from his comments in the Conference and published in his written report, we learn that these images exist in the astral realm. We can also see that these seven seals are similar to some of the powerful imagery presented in the Book of Revelation. We learn that such images as these seals depict, are formed in the astral realm (by initiates, or by spiritual

Powers), so that they may be accessible to souls who are either empowered seers, such the writer of Revelation and Rudolf Steiner; or to souls who have the ability to glimpse prominent images in the astral realms.

We also note that in 1890, an occultist, Eliphas Levi, published in one of his books, six roughly drawn images which have some similarities to six of these seven seals. (Since the seventh seal is missing in his book, one could conclude that Levi did not perceive the astral imagery which make up the seventh seal). Rudolf Steiner avoids referring specifically to Levi, and says only, as quoted above, "...some of our seals correspond with that which can be found in this or that book; but others do not correspond." This was presumably done in order not give people reasons to wrongly conclude that he had any debt to Levi, in regard to these images.

That these images are referred to as 'seals' is not explained by Rudolf Steiner, but we can conclude that the reason is, that this word helpfully brings to mind, a parallel to what happens when, in this physical world, a person of power and wealth wants to create an image (usually the sign of their authority) so that others can see it. Their seal or image is carved in brass, and then pressed into soft wax, thereby leaving its imprint as a 'seal' in the cooling, solid wax. Likewise, when high spiritual Powers want to preserve important 'signposts' about the deep mysteries of existence, they create images which are imbued with powerful energies, keeping it in the astral realms for as long as it is needed. The few references to such 'seals' found in ancient Greek texts, indicate that a seal also carries in itself the spiritual essence of the astral reality that it symbolizes.

Editorial clarification added
Since Rudolf Steiner's comments are often very brief, it has been helpful to insert some additional words to make his meaning clearer: these are in italics and within brackets (*like this*). Also, because the lecture notes are corrupted in places, it has been necessary to insert a **Note** in the text from Rudolf Steiner, for the sake of clarity; these are written in this kind of font.

Rudolf Steiner's introduction to the purpose of the seven seals

In his written report of the 1907 Munich Conference about these seals, Rudolf Steiner writes:

They present in pictorial form very specific experiences of the astral realm. There is a definite significance to these images. At first many people seeing them will consider such images to be customary (*astral-esoteric*) symbols. But they are much more than that. Whoever wants to explain what is presented in them simply with their intellect, as allegories, has not entered into the spirit of them. One should *experience* with all of one's soul, the content of these seven images, with the undivided heart and mind. One should try to visualize in one's mind the details of the images, as strongly as one can: their form, colour and inner content, in such a way that one lives inwardly in the resulting 'Imagination' (*i.e., astral thought-forms arising from them*).

For their content corresponds to quite specific astral experiences of the seer. That which the seer wants to express in these images is not in any way at all an arbitrary symbol, or a dull allegory, but instead something which one can at best show by using a comparison. Consider a person who is in a room which is so illumined that on one wall his shadow is visible. This shadow-figure is in some ways similar to the person, who is casting the shadow. But it is in reality a two-dimensional image of a three-dimensional person. Just as a shadow has some relation to the person, so too, that which is depicted in the apocalyptic seals is related to certain experiences of the seer in the astral realm. The seals present silhouettes of the astral processes – 'presented' is meant in the sense of being transferred over from the reality to a pictorial image. Therefore also, they are not (*simply*) graphics personally chosen by someone; but rather (*as important depictions of dynamics underlying humanity's evolution, displayed as images in the astral realm*) everyone who knows these spiritual dynamics, can discover them in the physical world, (*when they are depicted*) in their silhouette (*that is, as these seals*).

One cannot artificially devise such contents as this; rather one takes this from the available teachings of Esoteric Knowledge. Someone who has acquaintance with these topics could observe that some of our seals correspond with what can be found in this or that book; but others do not correspond. The cause of this situation is that some of the 'Imaginations' (*i.e., astral thought-forms*) of Esoteric Knowledge have already been communicated in books; but other content has not been published. Actually it is only possible now in our times for the most important and true Esoteric Knowledge to become publicly available. A part of theosophical tasks has to include making available to people much of that which, up until now, has been strictly kept secret by those appointed as guardians (*in un-named European esoteric circles*). This situation demands that the spiritual-cultural life of our times is (*nurtured and*) developed by the people who are the bearers of (*true*) Esoteric Knowledge.

The evolution of humanity is depicted in these seals: the expression of this evolutionary process, in the astral realm, forms one of the most essential bases of esoteric knowledge. The Christian esotericist will recognize them as being to some extent present in the images found in the Book of Revelation. But the form in which these are offered in our festive hall corresponds to the stream of esoteric knowledge which has been the primary stream of the western world since the 14th century. (*That is, a nuance is given to these seals from 'Rosicrucian' wisdom.*)

Such secrets of existence as are conveyed in these images, represent very ancient wisdom: the seers in the different epochs of humanity's evolution see this wisdom from different viewpoints. For this reason, the form in which they are presented changes according to the requirements of the various evolutionary epochs. In the book of Revelation by St. John (1:1), it is written, "a sign is given as to what should happen soon".

Those people understand how to correctly read a literary expression of Esoteric Knowledge (*such as is given in the Book of Revelation*), who realize that these words from Revelation are nothing other than a reference to these graphic symbolic images of Esoteric Knowledge (*that is, the seals*). The seals can be experienced in the astral realm, and then the seer knows that they are about (*the deeper secrets of*) the human being – in so far as this is unveiled in (*any given epoch of*) time (*from initiation wisdom*)...

The surrounding red colour

The circular seals were painted within a strong, vivid red surrounding. In his written report of the 1907 Munich Conference, Rudolf Steiner explained:

The conference hall was decorated by us so as to have a strong, stimulating, red colour as the predominating colour of all the walls. This colour is there to bring into external expression the prevailing mood of our festive gathering. It is quite clear that many objections to the use of red for this purpose could be made. And so long as one bases one's argument on exoteric assessments and experience, then these objections would be valid. To the esotericist, these objections are known, but who nevertheless, in harmony with all esoteric symbols, has to use the red colour for the purpose intended here. For the esotericist, it is not a matter of going along with what that part of his or her nature feels, in respect of the immediately perceptible sensory environment, but with what the Higher-self can experience, in its creative interaction in the spirit.

And this is exactly the opposite of what are the usual feelings about 'red'. For esoteric cognizance says: "If you want to attune your innermost being in the way that the gods' inner nature was attuned as they bestowed the green mantle of plants upon the world, then learn to endure 'red' in your environs as the Gods had to endure (*it*)".... Below, there is green as signifier of the Earthly element; above is there is red, as signifier of the heavenly creator-powers (the Elohim).

> **Note**: "endure (*it*)": the German text is ambiguous here, but the word "it" almost certainly refers in fact to the green colour (of the earthly plant-world), and not to 'red'. In terms of colours, in the specific context of Gods creating the earthly world, thus green, a main colour of the environs, this would have been for the sun-gods quite alien, for green is the colour of physical substances when permeated by etheric energies; predominantly the Earth's flora. (We can allocate colours to different places and realms, depending on the perspective of the moment; it is a flexible situation.) It is very relevant here to note that red is the colour used by Rudolf Steiner, in the large cupola of the Goetheanum for the 'colour-cloud' from which the sun-gods, the Elohim, or Powers, are manifesting, when they are creating the earthly world: exactly the context of this lecture. This perspective, of green representing the earthly reality, also underlies the colour sequence for the Goetheanum windows.
>
> In his first informal lecture on the seals, (21st May, 1907) in Munich, Rudolf Steiner spoke firstly to the assembled guests about the reason for this red colour, bringing another perspective to the guests, different to what is written in his Report.

I wish to say a few words about the colour which we have used here. There is a good reason that it is red. As you view it, this colour forms its counter-colour in your inner being; for the eye has the tendency to produce the counterpart, bluish-green, when you are gazing at red. This is (*due to*) the inner (*etheric*) activity of the eye. Regarding children, (*their response to colours)* very much depends upon how the body responds to outer sensory impressions. I'm speaking here now, in what I'm saying about the colour red, from the viewpoint of education.[1] The eye responds to a red-coloured environment with the tendency towards a green-blue colour: and this inner activity has a calming effect. For this reason, the colour red has a calming effect on overly excited children....

Our inner nature must become as ethereally pure as the cosmic ether above us; this ether which meets us in the blue colour (*of the firmament*). Hence educational activity makes use of this process, in the red colour of our surroundings (*here in this hall*). If red envelops us externally, then as a consequence, the counter colour of red lives in our inner being. It is on this basis that red is present in all sacred sites of the esotericists, whilst in exoteric sacred places where the secret wisdom is presented (*indirectly*) in an external way, including in symbols, blue is the predominant colour used. But the Rosicrucian world-view is expressed in the red colour (*used here*). If this

---

[1] Earlier in this informal session, the question of the education of the child was discussed.

space were to be fully furnished in accordance with the Rosicrucian world-view (*regarding the soul influence of colours*), then there should also be blue-coloured arcs up above us.

> **Note**: Another explanation of the impact of the colour red on the soul, which presents a different perspective, was given by Rudolf Steiner in connection with a small building in the Stuttgart area, in the town of Malsch, designed to be a kind of small esoteric meeting place,

If we look (*out into the sense-world*) within a glowing pure red, we come into contact with a special kind of elemental being. We encounter beings whose work provides the most beneficial energies for the future of humanity's existence on the Earth...through this influence the human being can become ever more chaste in their bloodstream, that is, in regard to the lower passions. (GA 284-5 lect. 15th Oct. pm, 1911)

Cautionary words from Rudolf Steiner:

In the following lecture extract, he cautions that the images of the seals, set up in the hall, have a spiritual power which, if displayed in normal everyday settings, may have a harmful effect. They must be kept only in a space reserved for contemplating spiritual truths.

"You can convince yourselves that these images do exert an (*ennobling*) influence (*on the soul*). But they can also exert a very bad influence. These images exist in order to lead the human being into the most beautiful (*soul*) harmony. Those people who contemplate them in a truly theosophical(*-anthroposophical*) mood of soul, and in a place where the energies of the theosophical(*-anthroposophical*) life are flowing, shall find that these images have an effect which enlivens consciousness, and frees it (*from lower influences*). But if you were to hang up these images in the kitchen, for example, where they are viewed in the context of everyday thoughts, then they would cause deterioration in the body, right into the digestive system.

These images cannot be enjoyed with an unholy soul state, but only in the right mood of soul (*having reverence for sacred truths*). From these words, you can see that where there is powerful light, there can also be powerful shadows.

But nevertheless, one may not denigrate esoteric wisdom, if a strong darkness falls on someone who does the wrong thing with such sacred esoteric images....Theosophy(-*Anthroposophy*) is not a game with intellectual ideas, rather it is a real power, a power which must flow into the cultural-spiritual life of humanity.

For this reason, one may not play games with such images, with such wisdom; rather one has to be fully aware that these are realities, which exert a real, actual influence on the soul.

(19th Oct. Berlin 1907 GA284/5)

SEAL ONE

The Son of Man, the Ancient of Days:

The Logos manifesting through the future human being

What do we see there ?

A glowing white figure of a man, in motion, as if dancing.

His right hand is encircled by astrological symbols of the seven classical planets.

Very prominent is a fiery, sword-shaped energy raying forth from his mouth.

Twelve burning oil-lamps are positioned around the perimeter of the black border.

Around his waist is a golden sash.

As Rudolf Steiner's explanatory words point out, this seal is alluding to the fiery, divine Will slumbering within the human being. In the Beginning (the Saturn Aeon) this Will rayed forth from the Logos, creating the germinal seed-bud of human beings; this is referred to in the Prologue to the Gospel of St. John. Then at the end of the seven Aeons, this divine 'spark' shall have been raised to consciousness in human beings, and shall manifest through the human voice.

My commentary clarifies these inspiring themes. We see how this seal could be called the "Alpha and the Omega". It is indicating the future emerging into consciousness of the divine potential in the human being; a potential which was rayed forth from the Logos in primordial times, and is now slumbering the depths of the human being's will.

Rudolf Steiner's explanation of Seal 1

Note: Only those sections from his brief explanations written for the Folio published in October 1907 are included which do not duplicate what is said in the three other sources.

A: Written report of the 1907 Munich Conference (from GA 34, p. 593-99)

The first seal represents the entire evolutionary path of humanity, in the most general sense. The theme of this seal is alluded to in the Apocalypse of St. John, with these words, (1:12-16)

> "And when I turned around, I saw seven golden lamp stands, and in the midst of these lamp stands, there was one like unto the Son of Man, dressed in a robe reaching down to his feet and with a golden sash around his chest.
> His head and hair were white like wool, as white as snow, and his eyes were like blazing fire.
> His feet were like bronze glowing in a furnace, and his voice was like the sound of rushing waters.
> In his right hand he held seven stars, and out of his mouth came a sharp double-edged sword, and his eyes were as radiant as the Sun shining in all its brilliance."

With such words, comprehensive secrets of humanity's evolution are being indicated, in general terms. If one wanted to present in a detailed way, what each of these significant words contain, I would have to write a large book. Our seal presents the significant meaning of these words in a pictorial way. Only a few indications can be given now. Amongst the bodily organs and kinds of 'gestures' (*which various shapes and actions*) of the human body display, there are those 'gestures' which, in their contemporary form, display the retrograde developmental stages of earlier forms. These are ones which have already passed beyond the perfected state of their forms, {*and are hence now in decline*}. Whereas other bodily organs present just the beginnings of their development; they are now only the basic foundation, so to speak, of what they shall become in the future. The esotericist has to know these secrets of humanity's evolution.

One organ which shall be something much higher, much more perfected, in the future than it is now, is the organ for speech. When one reveals this, one is touching on a great secret of existence: a secret which is often referred to as the "Mystery of the creative Word". Thereby an indication is given about the future state of the human speech organ. In the future, when human beings have become spiritualized, this organ shall be a spiritually productive, creative organ.

In myths and religion this spiritual bringing-forth is indicated by an appropriate image of a sword coming out of the mouth. Thus, every line, every point of the seal signifies that which is connected with the secret of human evolution. That such images were created, does not just arise from the need to depict (*transcendent*), spiritual processes, but because it is the case that these images correspond in a symbolic way to spiritual reality. And 'living-into' these images - assuming that they are valid images - has the effect that (*cognitional*) forces are aroused, forces which are slumbering in the human soul. Moreover, the creating of such images {*by initiates or spiritual beings*} tells us that this process of 'living-into' these graphic pictures does enable images about the spiritual worlds to arise (*that is why these seals are created*).

It is not actually the correct approach, when in Theosophy(-*Anthroposophy*) the higher realms are described only in schematic, diagrammatic ways. The true way is that pathway, through which such images are brought into consciousness as those in these seals. If the esotericist does not have such graphic pictures to hand, then he or she should give verbally (*to their students*) a description of the spiritual worlds in appropriate graphic pictures.

B: Explanation given in the 1907 Munich Conference.

Lecture of 21st May 1907

First Seal

The main feature is that of a man with the fiery sword in his mouth. This sword - and this feature is a primary aspect of the figure - is connected to a secret of evolution. Speech has always been compared to the sword. This is not simply a poetic image. In esoteric matters, everything has to be understood literally. But one has to then understand how to interpret this. There exists a certain secret connection between what exists in our speech - and which comes to expression through our larynx - and the current lower human reproductive urges. The human form is in a process of metamorphosis. Many people can already see this in the astral realm. A condition which the human being shall attain in the future can be seen by the clairvoyant in such an image as the first of our seven images. This image exists today in astral form. It is presenting an evolutionary condition of the human body, in the future.

If we wish to visualize this condition, then we have to think of it in such a way that we say: through the current lower reproduction power, the human being brings into action a productive activity within the instinctive and unconscious soul-life. Through the reproductive urge, the human being can bring forth forms filled with physical matter (*that is, a physical-material embryo*). But in the human being there exists another power, which cannot as yet enable the human being to bring forth permanent forms (*i.e., an object which continues on as a real thing, but not necessarily made of matter*); this is the power of speech. In that I am speaking here, I am producing something. If you were to investigate what happens in this space, whilst I am speaking, you would be examining vibrating air waves. The air waves are nothing else than 'moving words' (*air wave patterns in motion*). It was such movements in the air (*and the ether*) created by words (*spoken by the gods*), which, in remote Ages, manifested what the reproductive power manifests today. (*With the Gods, it was actual etheric objects, which eventually condensed into physical-material objects as the Earth hardened; with humans, it is real material-physical embryos*).

What is condensed today, was once, when it was still spirit, words set in motion. What the human being can only produce today from words, something in motion in the air, shall later become a truly reproductive power. Just consider that, if you were able to make my moving words become stationary, so that the air waves, having congealed, were to fall down towards the ground, you would find that for every word an especial form (*is to be seen*). For the word 'and' there would be a different form, than for the word, 'God'; perhaps the form of a mussel, or whatever. So when I speak the word 'God', a different form would be precipitated, than for the word 'and'. Esoteric wisdom shows us that everything around about us, as physical objects, was actually created (*i.e., precipitated*) in this same way. The spirit of the Logos resounded in space (*long Ages ago*) and (*eventually*) tenuous matter was formed; then a congealing process occurred, (*hardening this matter*). What today we have all around us, are words manifesting as forms: condensed divine words. The powers in us are condensed divine forces.

> Note: The above sentence is obscure, it is probably incomplete. It appears to mean; not only are the physical forms of our body condensed 'words' of the Gods, but the physical energies which are present in the muscles and the body generally, and also the subtle etheric energies in the body, are derived from the Ideas or 'words' of the Gods.

What in earlier Ages was created by the Word, has now become fixed in natural (*physical*) forms (*in our environment*). So, in the future course of evolution, the human larynx shall become a reproductive organ. Then we shall be able not only to produce[2] movements (*in the air and ether*), but the larynx will become a true reproductive organ. What today is speech, shall then be a power which brings forth its own kind. The larynx is the future reproductive organ, but raised up into a spiritual state of being; this is why with males, there is the parallel between the maturing of a sexual capacity and the developing of the larynx. With the change in the voice of boys at puberty there is a pointer to the creative power, which shall develop in the future from out of the voice.

The true reproductive power shall arise from speech; a conscious 'begetting power'. And you know that we give the name 'Fire-spirits' (*or Archangels*) to the spiritual beings who were at the same evolutionary stage in the ancient Sun aeon, as we are in this Aeon[3]. We do this because these beings were experiencing the same living interaction with the fiery element, as we are experiencing today, but with the air. (*In the Sun Aeon the Archangels were breathing-in the fiery, vaporous misty 'atmosphere' surrounding the primordial Earth of that aeon.*) It shall happen that, in the future ascending cycle of evolution, we shall progress from the state of being 'air entities' up to that of 'fire beings'. Then, from the throat, there shall stream forth not only a (*general, spiritual*) power, but also that power which today is the especial quality of the Fire-spirits (*Archangels*). (*This is the Life-spirit or 'Buddhi', that is, divine etheric forces.*)

You see depicted in the first seal, in the fiery sword of this figure, that which represents the eternal nature of the human being - that aspect of the human being which goes through all the incarnations. This eternal part of the human being is also the divine Creative Principle. It is true that the part of us which goes through all the incarnations, is of the same nature as that which has created the sevenfold planetary sequence. For this reason the man depicted here holds the symbols of the seven planets in his right hand.

C: Lecture of 16th September 1907

First Seal

The first seal depicts a human being clothed with white garments, and having feet like metal, similar to bronze. From out of his mouth comes a fiery sword, his right hand is encircled by the seven planets: Saturn, Sun, Moon, Mars, Mercury, Jupiter, and Venus. Those who are familiar with the Apocalypse of St. John know that in this book a somewhat similar description of this figure is found; for John was an initiate. One

---

[2] 'produce': the verb used here in German 'erzeugen' also has the meaning , 'to beget'.

[3] Here the text has only these brief words, "you know, that to the beings who were our predecessors..." The reference is actually to the Archangels, who in the Sun aeon, were at our 'human' stage; that is, having a personal ego-sense.

could say that this seal depicts the Idea behind humanity as such. We shall understand this when we call to mind some concepts which the older Members here already know.

When we go back in humanity's evolution, we arrive at a time when the human being existed at a very imperfect stage. For the human being then did not as yet have what you all carry on your shoulders: the head. It would sound really grotesque to you, if a description were given of the human being of a remote Age. For the head had to develop very gradually, and it shall continue to evolve. There exist organs in the human being today which are, so to speak, at the end of their evolution. In the future these shall no longer be in the body, whereas there are other organs which shall metamorphose; the larynx is such an organ. This has a mighty future ahead of it; this future stage is in fact connected with the heart.

Today, the larynx is at the beginning of its evolution, in the future, it shall be the spiritually transformed reproductive organ. You can gain an idea of this mystery when you are clear about what is brought about by the larynx today. In that here I am speaking, you hear my words. In that this hall is filled with air, and in this air certain vibrations are called forth, my words are carried along to your ears. When I speak a word, for example 'world', waves cause vibrations in the air - these are embodiments of my words. That which the human being of today brings forth in this manner, is called, (*in esotericism*), 'the bringing-forth in the mineral realm'. The movements of the air are mineral movements; (*i.e., movements affecting material substances, or inert, chemical-molecular substances; these are 'mineralized matter'*). Through the larynx, the human being exerts an influence in the mineral realm.

> Note: We can see here that in this Conference, where for the first time the Arts were being properly valued in an esoteric-spiritual context, the participants were being given a chance to gently encounter the conceptual basis of what we now know as the art of eurythmy; but which in 1907 had not yet been taught.

But the human being shall ascend (*in its evolutionary status*) and in the future, exert its influences in a plant-like manner (*into the etheric environment*). Then the human being shall not only be exerting a mineral(*-physical*) influence, but also be calling forth vibrations connected to, or resonating with, plants. The human being shall then 'speak forth plants'. The next step will be that the human being shall 'speak forth' sentient (astral) beings, and then, on the highest step, the human being shall speak forth beings of its own human status. Just as now the human being can only speak forth the inner context of his or her own soul, in this highest stage, the human being shall speak forth his or her own self. And just as the human being in the future shall speak forth *beings*, likewise gods, in the remote past, were endowed with an organ with which they 'spoke forth' all things which today exist. The gods have spoken forth all human beings, all animals, and everything else. All these beings and things are 'spoken-forth divine words', in a literal sense. (*At the beginning of the Gospel of St. John we read,*)

> "In the beginning was the Word, and the Word was with God, and a god was the Word."

This is not a philosophical statement in the speculative sense, for St. John has placed there (*in the beginning of his Gospel*) a primal reality, which is to be taken literally. And at the end (*of time*) there shall exist the Word; for Creation is a bringing into reality of the Word. And what the human being of the future shall bring forth, shall be a realization of (*the full potential of*) that which today is (*simply*) a 'word'. But then the human being shall no longer have such a physical form as we have today. It shall then have progressed to that form which existed in the Saturn (*aeon*); that is, to 'fire-substance'.

> Note: the above sentence is corrupted, giving a misleading, retrograde nuance to our future. Bearing in mind that Divine Will is classically described as manifesting as 'fire', there were probably two sentences, like these: "Human beings shall progress up to the state of being capable of consciously integrating, or resonating with, the divine Will-force. As a result, human beings shall progress up to a tenuous bodily form having a similar permeation by Divine Will, as our bodily form had, in the Saturn Aeon."
> This same divine Will also provided the basis of our will capacity. It was this divine fiery energy (*rayed-forth by the Thrones*) which provided the basis of the tenuous, subtle, bodily form of the human being, which existed in the Saturn Aeon.

That being who has spoken forth everything into the world which today is in it: this deity (*the Logos*) is the great archetype of the human being. This deity has spoken forth into the universe, the evolutionary Aeons: Saturn, Sun, Moon and Earth - in its two halves, Mars and Mercury - and Jupiter and Venus. The seven stars represent these (*aeons*); they are a signifier as to what heights the human being can evolve itself. At the end of the evolutionary cycle, the Earth shall be formed of 'fire-substance'; and the human being will be able to speak in a creative way in this 'fire-substance'. This is the 'fiery sword', which proceeds forth from the man's mouth. Everything will then be fiery; hence the feet are formed of molten bronze.

D: From the brief explanation in the October Folio (relevant sections)
......In myths and in religious accounts, this future spiritualized 'generative-form' is indicated by the **appropriate** image of the fiery sword coming from the mouth. The first stages of evolution of humanity upon the (*physical*) Earth occurred in a time when the Earth was still in a fiery state; and the (*bodily vessels for the*) first incarnations of human beings were shaped and formed from the element of fire. At the end of their earthly course of lives, (i.e., *when reincarnation ceases*) human beings shall have their own inner nature raying out into the world around them; this shall be brought about through the power of this fire element.

This developmental progress, from the beginnings of the Earth unto the end of the Earth, is perceptible to the seer when he or she gazes from within the astral realm upon the **Archetype** of the human being in the process of becoming. It is this which is portrayed in the first seal. The beginning of the Earth's developmental process is there in the fiery feet, the end is there in the fiery countenance; and the spiritual power of the "Creative Word" which is to be attained, is shown there in the fiery sword, which proceeds from the mouth.....

(Word in bold fonts emphasized by Rudolf Steiner)

COMMENTARY: SEAL ONE

To the written Report:

"a sign is given as to what should happen soon".

The NIV translation of Revelation1:1 is, "The revelation of Jesus Christ, which God gave him to show his servants what must soon take place." The words quoted by Rudolf Steiner are actually a mixture of the usual versions and his own more esoteric, more insightful translation. Rudolf Steiner specifically explains in his later lectures on the Apocalypse from 1908, that the accepted translations are incorrect to the meaning of this sentence. In his 1908 lectures, he offers his own, more insightful, translation:

> "This is the revelation of Jesus Christ, which God has given to His servant, presenting this to His servant in a brief, symbolic manner, as images."

It is clear from his radically different translation, that Rudolf Steiner is saying in his lecture at the Munich Conference that the potent imagery in the Book of Revelation is serving the same function as these Apocalyptic Seals.[4]

The Son of Man

The figure in the seal relates to a very important scene placed at the beginning of Revelation, in which this image is identified as The Son of Man. Since this Son of Man image is a key theme in the two other lectures about the seals, it will be discussed here. The esoteric image presented in the first chapter of the Book of Revelation, and identified as "The Son of Man", is not unique to that book. It was already in existence as an esoteric, unexplained figure in the Book of Daniel, where a clairvoyant, initiatory experience of a very similar spiritual being occurs,

> Dan 7:9 "As I looked, thrones were set in place, and the Ancient of Days took his seat. His clothing was as white as snow; the hair of his head was white like wool. His throne was flaming with fire, and ….."

Here the figure is not called the 'Son of Man', but "The Ancient of Days", a term which is not explained. Another similar reference, including both these figures, is in an esoteric text which dates to shortly before the time of Christ, *The Book of Enoch* (46:1-3):

> And there I saw One who had a Head of Days (*i.e., the Ancient of Days*)
> and his head was white like wool
> and with him was another being whose countenance had
> the appearance of a man
> and the face of this being was full of graciousness, like one of the holy Angels,
> And I asked the Angel (*who was guiding me*) who this being was, and
> from whence he came, and why he accompanied the Head of Days?
> And the Angel answered me and said,
> This is The Son of Man, he who has righteousness (*i.e., high spirituality*)….

[4] Rudolf Steiner's translation of the sentence from Revelation is fully correct to the Greek text, even though widely different from the usual versions; for example en tachsei (ἐν τάχει) can indeed mean "in a brief manner", not only "in haste"; but a detailed analysis of the Greek is not intended here.

We can see from these texts, that the nature of the spiritual entities known as "The Son of Man" and "The Ancient of Days", are closely linked together. We also need to bear in mind that Jesus himself is loosely identified with The Son of Man in the Gospels and in Revelation.

Exploring this topic takes us into deep secrets of initiation wisdom. It represents two very significant things. Firstly, the high clairvoyance or spiritual cognizing ability of initiates revealed to them that the matrix of the human spirit derives from the Logos. Secondly, the seal is indicating what the Logos, as its influence is taken up by divine hierarchical beings, intends the human being to become, in the far future. On the basis of these two points, this image is designed to tell us that the human being, in its future perfected state, shall dynamically manifest its ancient spiritual origins. In other words, what is currently slumbering in the human soul - the Logos - shall by then have awoken, for the human being shall be able to merge with, or identify with, these divine foundational energies.

This awakening of the future human being to the Divine within, is signified in the Book of Revelation (1:15), where it refers to the voice of The Son of Man in the same way that the voice of God is described in the Book of Ezekiel (43:1); that is, with "a voice of many rushing waters". Revelation has the future spiritualized human being (The Son of Man) speaking with exactly this same 'voice' as 'God' in Ezekiel. In fact the Greek text in Revelation, in its grammatical structure, is a precise copy of the Hebrew text of Ezekiel. It is for these reasons, that in Revelation, The Ancient of Days is described in a similar way to that of The Son of Man, who states "I am the Alpha and the Omega", or "The 'I am' is the Alpha and the Omega". That is, the true Higher-self or "I" of the human being has the Logos influence as its primordial 'ferment'; and over the aeons this sublime spiritual reality has become the very 'substance' of the redeemed spiritualized human being. So, The Ancient of Days figure is in effect a way of presenting the profound truth that 'God' is similar to the future perfected human being, in an inner sense. That is, God is the archetype of, or the matrix of, the human spirit.

The term 'God' in these esoteric texts refers in a general way to the Divine reality behind the cosmos, thus it encompasses Jahve and the sun-god Christ, (both of whom are Powers, or Spirits of Form) and also the Logos. But also, as we have seen above, these texts are pointing to human beings as the offspring of, and as a vessel of, Deity. Subtle indications of this are also to be found elsewhere in Scripture. For example in the Book of Ezekiel (1:26) is a detailed description of God enthroned amidst the four 'apocalyptic animals'. Ezekiel describes part of the figure seen in his vision as looking like 'glowing metal'; then he refers to 'the Glory of God' (Jahve) appearing above a throne of sapphire. Then of this deity, who is radiant with glory, Ezekiel writes,

> "high above, on the throne, was a figure like that of a man."

So here is a reference to the Ancient of Days, indicating that this mysterious aspect of God has a similarity to the human being. Thereby implying that God is the archetype of the future, perfected human being, known as the Son of Man, or on an even higher level, The Son of God. These terms are discussed below.

The Son of Man and the Son of God

Before we contemplate this seal further, it would be helpful to explain two core anthroposophical terms.

The **Spiritual-self** arises when the personal soul, with its emotions, intelligence and will, is refined and ennobled. As this happens, then the feelings or emotions become compassionate, chaste and gentle; the intellect loses its coldness, as influences from the heart (the emotions) warm and broaden it, causing intuitive ways of thinking to develop. Thirdly, the will is released from a narrow focus on self-centred goals, and become deeply social, wanting to help other people. In anthroposophical language, we could say that as the soul (or soul-body) is spiritualized, becoming ever more radiant, then the Spiritual-self arises. This means that the chakras have been brought into activity, bestowing various forms of higher consciousness (including clairvoyance) on the person. This in turn means that another aura, an aura consisting of 'devachanic' energies or light, grows and becomes ever more radiant.

The **Life-spirit** arises once the Spiritual-self is underway. As we develop even further towards spirituality than the Spiritual-self, it is possible for our ethereal energies, our 'ether-body' to be spiritualized. If that occurs, exceptional creative powers arise, and become active in the artistic field and in healing, and also as higher consciousness, that is, an advanced state of seership, beyond the astral realm. This Rudolf Steiner calls the **"Life-spirit'**. He once described this higher, spiritual part of us in this way,

> Visualize the usual life-forces now conserved by a pure, restrained harmonious life-style, and then made to resonate, to respond, to the utterly outpouring, selfless compassion of the Spirit-self.[5]

A detailed exploration of the nature of The Son of Man and The Son of God, as indicated in Biblical and extra-Biblical texts, is beyond the scope of this book, but we can consider the valuable explanations of these terms from Rudolf Steiner. He reveals that in the Mystery Centres or secluded esoteric groups of the Hellenistic Age, particular terms were decided upon amongst those with initiatory wisdom, to refer to various aspects of higher consciousness or stages of spiritual development. Those acolytes on the esoteric path who achieved a high level of spirituality, after years of purification and soul tribulations, could develop the 'spiritual-soul': a term which means the higher, intuitive consciousness that gives insights into spiritual truths, and also usually some visual clairvoyance.

This stage of development would often also bring about some subtle presence of the divine 'Spiritual-self' in the acolyte. The Spiritual-self brings what we refer to as 'holiness' to such a person, so the Spiritual-self can be regarded as a manifestation of the 'Holy Spirit', especially if some initial development of the Life-spirit has also begun in that person. Such acolytes were then permitted to undergo the 3-day 'sleep' process, deep in a hidden sanctuary. In this process, they would experience consciously the spiritual world and then return to their body, now an initiate. These now initiated souls were called a 'Son of Man'. If they progressed even further with their inner development and experienced being blessed by the descent upon them of divine spiritual influences from the spiritual worlds, then they were called a 'Son of God'.[6]

So the figure in the first seal is a broad, general image, portraying both the future Son of Man and the Son of God. This same figure can also be seen as alluding to 'God': that is, to the interweaving of divine 'being-ness' from which the human spirit derives. But it thereby offers to the spiritual seeker, when contemplating the first seal, a portrayal of the future human being as a conscious manifestation of the great, transcendent

---

[5] GA 54, lecture 15th Feb. 1906, p. 289.

[6] This particular use of these terms in the Age is taught by Rudolf Steiner in, for example, GA 97 lect. 2nd. Dec. 1906, GA 123 lect.11.Dec. 1910, and GA 94 lect. 5.Nov. 1906.

Logos, whose Word brought forth the cosmos and within the cosmos, over vast Ages, the human being as well.

The Future Human Being

It appears that the 'future time' to which the seal refers, can be applied to several stages of humanity's future. Let's observe firstly, that this human is depicted with a striking 'body gesture': that of a dancer.[7] Instead of a static figure, he is a dynamic figure in motion. This feature alludes to an inherent intense inner liveliness or preparedness for action, which is the primary feature of the will.

That the creative (i.e., reproductive) power is now in the speech, not in the reproductive organs, indicates that a future Age is being referred to; this can be understood as the next aeon, called the Jupiter Aeon. In this aeon the Spiritual-self shall be fully developed, and the Lower-self shall have been conquered; in addition, the integration of cosmic spiritual powers will have been achieved. It is this capacity to resonate with, and then integrate, high spiritual influences from the zodiac and the planets, which actually bring about the Spiritual-self. But also, this 'dancing' figure can be understood from another perspective: it is alluding to human beings in the 'Vulcan' aeon, of the far future.[8] The term Vulcan was chosen by Rudolf Steiner for this aeon because of the classical association in Greek myths of Vulcan or Hephaestos with fire. Vulcan was a deity associated with subterranean, elemental fire. Rudolf Steiner told one audience that after the 7th aeon, there shall arise a new cosmos, which will have as its foundation, the primordial spiritual-fire of the Logos; this shall be our cosmic 'environment' in the Vulcan aeon.[9]

Two particular Vulcan features are shown here: the feet of molten bronze and the 12 zodiac energies being depicted as burning lamps. These feet indicate that the foundational element of human consciousness shall then be an inner 'fiery' power - derived from consciously becoming a vessel of Divine Will, which shall then find expression in the human will. To discern the message of these 12 burning lamps, we need to remind ourselves that the will is best depicted, in terms of elemental energies, as fire. So here, the zodiac is depicted as fire (lamps), to indicate a future cosmos in which Divine Will is now fully permeating the cosmos: this Will is now the all-encompassing, and dynamically manifesting element of the 'environment' in which the human being shall exist.

The Burning Lamps

We noted earlier that in the Book of Revelation, it is implied that The Son of Man is closely linked to the risen Jesus Christ. So, both The Son of Man and The Son of God are a way of representing not only the general spiritual future of humanity, but also the influence of the Logos, or the cosmic Christ, in the spiritual evolution of humanity. The future human being shall reveal, in its nature, once it is perfected and spiritualized, the 'substance' of the Divine; especially of the 'Christ' Logos and of the great sun-god Christ. For, as the early esoteric Christians were aware, there are two high beings who have been given the title 'Christ': the high Logos (*as mentioned in the Prologue to the Gospel of Lazaros-John*) and also the highest of the Powers or sun-gods.[10] The 12 burning lamps indicate zodiac influences, and therefore the powers of

---

[7] A dancer: and possibly of a eurythmist, although eurythmy was not yet known.

[8] A useful overview of these 7 aeons of our evolutionary pathway, and the complex series of cycles within each of these, is given in my *Rudolf Steiner Handbook.*

[9] GA 60, lect. 16th Mar. 1911, p.473.

[10] This topic is presented and clarified in my *Rudolf Steiner Handbook.*

the 'Christ' Logos are now fully awakened in the soul. The radiant white hair and the blazing eyes allude to the spiritual influences from the sun-god Christ, as now awakened and empowered in the soul.

The Golden Sash
It is also possible that there is another reference in this seal to the human soul as imbued with divine 'Grace' that is, with influences from the sun-god Christ; this is the golden sash or girdle. In the Book of Revelation, this sash is specifically described as being wrapped around the upper chest of the person. This is an unusual feature, but in addition, the sash is made of gold. These two qualities are indicating an aspect of the initiatory path, namely that the heart area now fully manifests sacred spiritual forces – the Spiritual-self qualities. These forces derive from Christ, that is, the great sun-god; the leader of the Powers. Hence the heart chakra – the great 12-petalled sun-imbued centre of the astral body – is now fully developed.

However, in the sketch of the seal by Rudolf Steiner, the position of the sash is unclear. In the published version of the seal with its red background, the sash is clearly placed much lower, around the waist. But in the folio published in September 1907, the seals were drawn by a different artist, and reproduced in black and white. This folio, created at Rudolf Steiner's request, included a short 3-page text from him about the seals. In this later edition, the sash in Seal One is drawn higher up on the chest – near to the heart area. It is very likely that Rudolf Steiner would have seen, and given his approval to, these images of September 1907, before they were published. If so, this could mean that the magnificent coloured version displayed at the Munich Conference, namely Seal One, in regard to this detail, may have been incorrect.

But the situation is somewhat fluid, because in his written Report, Rudolf Steiner quotes the passage exactly from the Book of Revelation (Luther's version) stating that the sash was around the chest. But in his written Introduction to the October Folio, he gives in his own words, a free rendering of the passage in Revelation, and states that the sash was around the hips.

The Fiery Sword
As Rudolf Steiner explains, the fiery sword depicts the creative-reproductive power of the human being, which will be manifested in the far future through the larynx, the power of speech. Literature which likens the flow of speech to a sharp sword, is not unique to the Book of Revelation; there are examples from other Biblical and related literature. There are some passages in the Old Testament which refer to this imagery, and in the New Testament, the Epistle to the Hebrews (4:12) has a closely related usage;

> "For the Word of God is living and active. Sharper than any double-edged sword, it penetrates even to dividing soul and spirit, joints and marrow; it judges the thoughts and attitudes of the heart."

It is significant that this imagery was used in a mystical text written by the Essenes. Rudolf Steiner reports that the Christian apostles were actively associated with, and interested in, the Essenes. This Essene hymn is about spiritual development and how the Divine seeks to assist the spiritual seeker,

> "….To give knowledge to the Wise that they may comprehend…..the Eternal Insight that you established, before you created me. And You kept Your Law before me, and You confirmed Your Covenant for me: (*thereby*) strengthening the Covenant upon my heart…. You have opened my conscience, and

> strengthened me, to (*help me*) pursue the Ways of Truth....You made my mouth like a sharp sword, and opened my tongue to words of Holiness....." (4Q436)[11]

In this text, there appears to be awareness of the powerful enhancement of speech which the initiate can achieve, and which many human beings may achieve in the distant future. Since we know from Rudolf Steiner that a high initiate, known as Jesus Ben Pandira, was the leader of the Essenes for some years around 100 BC, we can conclude that the Essenes, as a significant esoteric group of the Hellenistic Age, did know both the special term 'The Son of Man', and that the symbol of this future human state included a sword-like power issuing from the mouth.

This imagery, where speech is represented as a sword, is also found in the Hellenistic apocryphal book, *The Wisdom of Solomon* (18:15,16):

> Thy mighty Word leaped down from Heaven, out of the royal throne.... bearing the sharp sword of Thy immutable decree....

This text is a primary part of the 'Wisdom' literature of the Hellenistic Judaic people, and its focus was the attainment of that higher, intuitive state of consciousness known in anthroposophy as the 'spiritual-soul', which seeks to advance sufficiently to allow some of the Spiritual-self to be present also. It is also the case that many ancient Greek sages referred to the similarities of speech to a sword. For example this saying was current amongst these sages, "Do not stir fire with a sword".[12] This was understood to mean, do not provoke an already angry person with one's speech, and was mentioned by Pythagoras, Iamblichus, Plutarch and others.

The Seven Planetary symbols

The seven symbols of the planets are arranged in the correct sequence for the days of the week; there may be two reasons for this. Firstly, the planetary sequence points us to the influence in the soul of the planets themselves; the implication being, that the future spiritualised human being will have absorbed the finer astral influences from the planetary spheres, and expelled the lower astral influences. This is very significant, as the soul (or astral body) is actually composed of these planetary influences; so as these influences are ennobled, the soul itself is ennobled. Rudolf Steiner refers briefly to planetary qualities in regard to these symbols in his lecture at the Conference. (Consequently, as a later seal indicates, the Lower-self or Double of the human being can be viewed as sevenfold.)

The Finger of The Son of Man

The other reason for these seven images, and the one which Rudolf Steiner specifically mentioned in his lecture at the Conference, is that it directs our contemplations to humanity's evolution through the seven aeons. One notes that the index finger of the man's right hand is pointing towards the symbol for Saturn. It is valuable to contemplate this pointing towards Saturn together with the words of the 'The Son of Man' figure in the Book of Revelation (1:18b), "...I am the First and the Last...."

The reason for these details in the seal is to be found in the description by Rudolf Steiner in his *An Outline of Esoteric Science* which provides a description of the origin of Creation, and the evolution of humanity. He reveals how evolution proceeds through

---

[11] Text (lightly edited by this author); and was published in *The Dead Sea Scrolls Uncovered*, R Eisenman & M. Wise, p.239 (Element Books, 1992)

[12] Explained by many writers including 'Hippolytos', in *Refutations*, Book 6.

a sequence of seven aeons. We have earlier noted that the remarkable figure in this seal represents a distant future attainment by human beings of their spiritual potential: the Spirit-human or Atma or Atman quality. To understand why the seal is directing our attention to the seven aeons, we need to explore further the nature of the Atman or Spirit-human.

The Atma or Spirit-human

It was in the distant past, in the Saturn Aeon, that the intention of the Logos was received and worked with by the Thrones in particular, so that humanity would gradually come into being, at first only in a rudimentary form. Humanity in the Saturn Aeon consisted only of an archetypal thought-form and the tenuous, invisible energy-template of what later became the physical body. But hovering above that tenuous form was the Spirit-human or Atma, in an un-awakened state. That is, the Atma slept within the being-ness of the sublime Thrones, (although its origin is in the Logos, as the agent of the Father-God). But in the seal, this figure represents the end-point of humanity's evolution, that future Age where the conscious Atma is manifested.[13]

Looking at this evolutionary state more closely, we learn that before the rudimentary physical body was formed, an archetypal idea (*or archetypal form*) of the body had been developed, in the first level of Devachan. And from this, the template of the physical body was fashioned. This invisible energy template is called the 'phantom' by Rudolf Steiner and is itself directly linked to the devachanic archetype. But also the seventh, the highest part of our nature, the divine 'Spirit-human' or Atma was then created as a potential entity. It was not yet linked to an individual ego, since this did not exist in that remote Age. So in effect, even today, the Atma remains primarily unawakened, and this already indicates the purpose and highest future outcome of creation, namely that human beings may awaken the Atma or Spirit-human from within their ego-sense, that is as consciously striving individuals. This is the highest aspect of our spirit. We then become aligned to the will of 'God'.

A powerful description of this presence of divine will-forces behind the physical body, and therefore also forming a substantial, but sub-conscious, matrix of the human being's own will, is given in this report of Rudolf Steiner's teaching to a small group:

> "If the acolyte descends, with a clairvoyant consciousness or higher perceiving ability, into the inner nature of the physical body, there he or she finds an entire world of energies which are active within the will....these energies derive from divine beings who during the Saturn aeon poured-forth from their own spiritual nature, what we now know as the Will of the human being..."[14]

A series of profound meditations were given by Rudolf Steiner on the theme of the aeons. These are verses expressing reverence for the Logos, because behind the activity of the hierarchical beings is the Logos; the Logos is understood to be directly expressive of the will of the Father-God. Below is the meditation verse for this first aeon; it is the result of profound initiatory insight into the origin of the Atma. Such insights become possible for that person in whom the Atma has begun to develop, and hence in whom the highest spiritual state of consciousness, or clairvoyance, has awakened and brought these insights. This highest consciousness state is called 'Intuition' by Rudolf Steiner. (I have found that a less ambiguous term for this clairvoyance is 'High initiation consciousness'),

---

[13] Our evolutionary pathway beyond the Vulcan stage was not discussed by Rudolf Steiner.

[14] GA 265, p. 265.

SATURN AEON

Great, encompassing Spirit, * (* the Logos)
Thou who en-filled endless space,
when of my body's limbs
nothing was as yet existing.
    Thou wert. (* 'thou wert' is old style for = 'you were')
I raise my soul to thee.
I was in thee.
Thou didst emanate forces from thyself * (*via the Thrones)
and at the Earth's primordial beginning * (The Saturn Aeon)
was mirrored the first archetype of my bodily form.
Within the energies sent out from Thee was I myself.
    Thou wert.
My archetype intuited thee:
It intuited me: myself,
I, who was a part of thee.
Thou wert.

A meditative engagement with this verse reveals an almost 'koan-like' Zen quality, in that it points to dynamics which transcend logical thought-processes. Note that the word 'intuited' in the last lines involves a higher type of what we generally call 'intuition'; namely a state of cognizing which is defined by Rudolf Steiner with the word 'Intuition'; but in anthroposophical literature this term means a high devachanic level of consciousness. However, here 'intuition' has to be referring to this consciousness as it existed long ago in the Saturn Aeon. Back then, in its primordial, beginnings, humanity existed in a dreamless sleep state, pulsing within a cosmic matrix in which the potential future human being was immersed.

So in that remote time the human being was not consciously able to undertake any cognizing, as no ego had developed. So the 'intuiting' referred to here is the inherent state of the Atma, but there was actually no 'person' there as yet, to 'personally' be aware of this. To achieve 'Intuition' or 'high initiation consciousness' as ego-endowed human beings, is the great future task awaiting the spiritual seeker. Valuable help in this task is given in Rudolf Steiner's *Foundation Stone Meditation.*[15]

Commentary on Lecture, 21st May 1907

Various themes mentioned in the lecture have been explored in the above Commentary on the written report, but one further point in this lecture needs some clarification,

The Eternal part of the human being

"This eternal part of the human being is also the divine Creative Principle. It is true that, the part of us which goes through all the incarnations, is of the same nature as that which has created the sevenfold planetary sequence."

These words are indicating some especially deep truths. The part of the human being which "goes through all the incarnations" is initially the Spirit-self and especially the Life-spirit. The Life-spirit is the divine devachanic essence of our etheric body, but it arises on the basis of the Spiritual-self, which is the redeemed or purified, ennobled astral body. In this 'eternal part' of the human being, is contained the memory of all

---

[15] See the author's "*The Foundation Stone Meditation - a new Commentary*' for more about this.

our past incarnations. This part of human nature is also known as 'the Causal-body'. In the lecture Rudolf Steiner also informs his audience that this Causal-body "is of the same nature as that which has created the sevenfold planetary sequence". These words are indicating that we are 'a microcosm of the macrocosm'; that is, our astral body or soul is a replica, in miniature, of the planetary spheres. Which means, a miniature of the astral qualities of which the planetary system is composed. Here it is important to note that in Revelation the Saviour is presented as the person who has the seven planets in his right hand, indicating that Jesus Christ is the 'embodiment' of the perfected soul, for the highest planetary qualities are within his being. This is another meaning of the 'The Son of Man".

Commentary on Lecture 16th September 1907

Various themes mentioned in the lecture are already explored in the Commentary on the Written Report, but one historical point in this lecture needs clarification. We are told that "John is an initiate". Although the author of Revelation has long been considered to be St. John, brother of James, this view is not universally held by theologians. Rudolf Steiner taught that the name 'John' here refers to Lazaros-John; so he is the writer of the Book of Revelation, and also of the Gospel of St. John, not the Apostle John. This theme is explored in detail in my book, "Rudolf Steiner on Leonardo's *Last Supper*".

SEAL TWO

The Four Group-souls, and the Lamb of God

What do we see here?

Around a central object, the famous four 'apocalyptic creatures' are portrayed: a lion, eagle, bull and (potential) human being.

In the centre is the "Lamb of God", a spiritual reality mentioned early in the Gospel of St. John (1:29) and then again many times in Revelation.

Surrounding these 5 figures is a multi-coloured circle. This is in fact the rainbow, but thought of as an entire circle, not just the arc which we normally see, as we stand on the ground and look upwards. If we were to see a rainbow from a high altitude, it would appear as a circle. But here is a rainbow seen from a different, non-earthly perspective; for the colours are in a reversed sequence to what is seen physically. This means that we are seeing it from the astral realm (as Rudolf Steiner indicates in his explanation of the 4th seal, from 21st May).

Around the perimeter of the seal, in the black border, are 12 symbols, referring to the zodiac influences.

This seal is a lesson about humanity rising above the animal astrality, with which we were so closely interlinked, in previous evolutionary ages.

Rudolf Steiner's explanation of Seal 2

A: Written report of the Conference in Munich (GA 34 p. 597)

The Second Seal
The second seal, with its corresponding features, represents the early evolutionary conditions of earthly humanity. This earthly humankind in primordial ages actually had not yet developed what we call 'individuality'. There was in existence for humanity in those ancient times, what the animal species still have today: a Group-soul. That person who today through clairvoyance, investigates and follows the evolutionary course of the old human Group-souls, can discover these four kinds of human Group-souls which are presented in the second seal, namely, the Lion, the Bull, the Eagle and the (potential) Human. In knowing this, we are facing the truth of that which is so often dryly explained as merely allegorical ideas.

B: Conference lecture: 21st May 1907

The Second Seal
The second seal depicts the so-called 'apocalyptic beasts': the Lion, the Eagle, the Bull, and the Human. We gain an idea of these creatures, when we remind ourselves that the animal of current times does not have an ego-soul (*or "I"-soul*), such as we have. The animal does not have its ego-soul on the physical plane; each separate animal has a connection to the collective ego belonging to that animal species. This is a similar situation to that of the separate members of the human being, regarding the over-all "I".

> **Note**: This last sentence is obscure. It probably means: how the separate 'members' of human consciousness – our thinking, feeling and will – are integrated into our sense of "I". That is, how our ego monitors and interrelates these three faculties to each other.

For this reason, we speak of the 'Group-soul' of animals, and if you (*clairvoyantly*) investigate these Group-souls, you find them on the astral plane. Now it is clear to every person (*in this Conference*) that humanity in its evolution, has also gone through conditions where that part (*of human nature*) which was on the physical plane, did not yet possess an I-soul. In the past, the human being also went through evolutionary conditions during which it belonged to a Group-soul. This happened at the same point of time when the human being descended down into the physical bodily state, and thus the Group-soul condition changed into (*a condition which made possible*) an individuated soul.

> **Note**: This sentence is referring to the ancient epoch when human beings were drawn down into a material, flesh body; no longer existing in tenuous bodies formed of streams of fiery warmth, gases and moist vaporous elements. It was some 18 million years ago, in the second half of the Lemurian Epoch, after the extrusion of the Moon, that these subtle, delicate human bodies began to become imbued with accretions of denser matter, forming protoplasm and later, cartilaginous substance, and finally after more millions of years, calcium-based skeletal material.

In the far future, the human being shall once again have a Group-soul, except this time, in a fully conscious manner; that is, conscious in a higher sense. The symbol for this Group-soul is portrayed in the second seal.

The unity in the far future is portrayed through the external forms of the Group-souls, which the human being had in earlier times.

> **Note**: It is difficult to find any meaning in the above sentence; it appears that a number of words are missing. Possibly the audience was told that the future unity of the spiritualizing branch of humanity is depicted by the Lamb – this is the 'Group-soul' of those human beings who shall work their way through to the Spiritual-self, which is only now developing within humanity. Whereas the ancient animal Group-souls have provided several shapes, which though primarily fashioning the appearance of several major animal species, have also contributed to the general appearance of human beings' physical and etheric bodies.

These Group-souls, out of which the human individual soul has emerged, consist of four kinds….

> **Note**: this sentence is also corrupted, for it ends with these words,
>
> "and into which the soul shall return".
>
> But this statement contradicts what Rudolf Steiner taught in this regard. He emphasizes that the human being shall not return into these animal Group-souls, except for those who fall into the evil branch of humanity in the future. And when this does occur, those souls shall merge into the degraded offspring of these otherwise noble Group-souls. This is explained in the 1908 lecture-cycle, *The Apocalypse of St. John.*[16] The animal Group-soul become incarnate in the next aeon, these entities do not merge with humanity.

That means, four specific astral groups. One of these is characterized by the way it still incorporates today rudiments of the Bull-soul, another by how it develops within itself the Lion-soul, the third by how it develops within the Bird-soul. The characteristic of the fourth Group-soul, is that, it is from this one that the primordial human being arose, and this allowed the individual to appear (*in the course of evolution*). This fourth 'creature' is that Group-soul which one defines as the (*potential, future*) 'human'. The human being has arisen from out of these four Group-souls, (*but it is from the fourth, the 'human' Group-soul that the higher human being of the future shall arise*).[17] The most advanced of the Group-souls (*is the fifth one, existing only as a germinal prototype*), this is already individualized on the astral plane as the (*spiritualized*) human soul (*of the future*). This is to be seen symbolized in the centre of the seal.

This is the Christ-soul, symbolized by the Lamb, which completes the other four Group-souls, (*see the Commentary for explanation of this obscure sentence*). Then you see the rainbow which envelops the entire image in seven colours: this is the creative Principle, in a second form.

---

[16] The teaching (in GA 120, 17.5.1910) that in the future, humanity shall 'draw up' (some) animal species out of their degraded state is not implying that these entities shall merge with the human soul.

[17] Another corrupted place, where these words again occur: "and shall return back to these, (in the future)".

Note: The 'second form' of the creative Principle (i.e., cosmic Power) appears to mean that this creative Principle was firstly depicted, in the first seal, as a fiery ray, whereas now it is depicted as a rainbow. These are actually two quite different aspects of the same divine creative power.[18]

This 'second form' is the rainbow, the sevenfold creative cosmic Principle (*i.e., Power*). (*See the commentary for more about this.*) This is what was active as the driving force in the foundations of humanity's evolutionary pathway, in the inner recesses of the soul (*not in the external appearance*). This occurred long ago, when the human being was at the stage of being part of a Group-soul.

Also, regarding the numerals from 1 to 12, placed around the periphery of the seal, which are to be viewed as hour markers around the coloured circles of the rainbow, we need to remind ourselves that long ago, Earth, Moon and Sun were one unitary body. Such spiritual dynamics as are presented here, should be seen as connected to this unity (*i.e., to this unified state*). Long ago, this unified configuration of the cosmic order was necessary, so that the human being could exist as a Group-soul.

Note: The Earth, Moon and Sun were one unified celestial body in the ancient Polarian and Hyperborean epochs; both these epochs preceded the Lemurian epoch. In those epochs the Earth had not yet descended down to the mineralized condition, and hence had no hardened matter in its tenuous physical body. The Moon was not a distinct entity; it was part of the over-all primordial Earth. It was not until mid-Lemurian times, that the (future) Moon's substances, which were widely diffused in the Earth, were gathered into one area, and then cast out of Earth, becoming a satellite.

Our current divisions of time are connected with the relation of cosmic (*astronomical*) bodies to each other. In that primordial Age when the Earth was not yet separated from, and not orbiting around, the Sun, all time factors had to be different to what they are today; back then there was no day and no night. The Sun itself however was in motion; there prevailed then a great cosmic clock-face, so to speak (*i.e., the sun moving through what would become the zodiac of our Age*). This portrayed the places which the Sun passed through. The hour-hand of our clocks today goes around the clock-face twice every day; in a similar manner, in that primordial cosmic time reckoning, the Sun journeyed not once, but twice around the zodiac; through a phase of brightness and a phase of darkness. This twofold passing through these stations along the way, esotericists called "the journeying-past of the Elder Brothers" in the cosmic Order. This is (*also what is meant by*) the "Twenty Four Elders" of the Apocalypse. In this way, a kind of cosmic clock was arranged, (*see the Commentary for more about this*).

C: Lecture of 16th September 1907

The Second Seal

When you compare the present-day human being with the animal, then the difference presents itself in such a way that one has to say: the human being, as an individual being, has within itself, that which each separate animal does not have. The human being has an individual soul; the animal has a Group-soul. The human being is in itself the equivalent of an entire animal species. For example, all lions together have only the

[18] The official English version, *Rosicrucianism Renewed*, omits both references to "a second form", (p 77).

one soul. This Group-soul is quite similar (*in level of attainment*) to the human "I", except that it has not descended down into the physical world; it is to be found only in the astral world. Here in the physical world, you see physical people, of which everyone has an "I". In the astral world you encounter beings in astral substance who are similar to yourself, except that they are not in physical sheaths, but astral sheaths. You can speak with them as you can with human beings: these are the animal Group-souls.

The human being also once had a Group-soul, but has gradually developed up to having the present-day independence. These Group-souls were originally in the astral world, but have descended (*into the physical world*) so as to dwell in the flesh. When one investigates these primal Group-souls of humanity in the astral world, then one finds four types from which the human being has originated. If one were to compare these Group-souls with those which belong to the present-day animal species, then one would have to say: one of the four can be compared to the lions, another to the eagles, a third to the cows, and the fourth to people of ancient times before the "I" has descended.

In this way, in the second seal, an earlier evolutionary stage of humanity is presented in the apocalyptic beasts: the Lion, the Eagle, the Bovine and the (*potential*) Human. But there also exists, and shall always exist, so long as the Earth itself exists, a Group-soul for the higher manifestation of the human being. This is portrayed by the Lamb, by the Mystical Lamb; the signifier of the Redeemer. This grouping together of the five Group-souls, that is, the four (*providing the earthly astrality*) of humanity and the great Group-soul to which all people (*who develop a higher astrality*) together belong: this what the second seal portrays.

D: From the brief comments in the October Folio

The Second Seal
(There are no additional comments about the seal in this text.)

COMMENTARY: SEAL TWO

The Rainbow representing a cosmic Creative Principle
Since the rainbow symbolizes the seven planets, these words are referring to the divine creative powers of the hierarchical beings who manifest through the planetary spheres. The astral qualities in these spheres are the source of humanity's own astral body; for we are a microcosm of the macrocosm. So whatever qualities the human soul possesses, derives from these planetary powers, from what they have rayed forth into primordial humanity, long ages ago. Rudolf Steiner taught that the planetary spheres relate to the sevenfold human being, below is the correlation of the planets to our soul.[19]

The link of the planets to the sevenfold human being

MOON: **life-forces** or the 'body' of etheric energies.
= the predisposition, moods, habitual attitudes

VENUS: the **emotions** and also the **Spiritual-self**
= desires, yearnings, romantic-love, artistic abilities and spirituality

MERCURY: **thinking**
= intelligence, cleverness: the intellectual-soul

SUN: **the ego** or our actual sense of self
= initiatives, decisions, attitudes

MARS: the **vehemence of the inner-life**
= the intensity of desires, and of feelings, thoughts, and will

JUPITER: **intuitive insights**, logical thinking, expansiveness
= joviality, deep poetry, wisdom: the spiritual-soul

SATURN: **subconscious Will**
= sensing of our life-purpose/karma, our spiritual matrix

The Lion, Eagle, Bull and (potential) Human
We need to gain a clear understanding of these famous 'four apocalyptic animals'. A useful starting point is these words from Rudolf Steiner,

> These four apocalyptic animals are the four types of Group-souls which the human being, in his or her individual soul, is closest to, in the astral realm.[20]

We also learn that as the fourfold human being was developed in evolution, these four Group-souls arose. The Bull came about as the physical-material body of the human being was forming, the Lion came about as the etheric body was forming, the Eagle likewise, as the astral body was forming; and finally as human beings gradually developed a human astral quality, even if long ago this was quite primitive, there arose a bodily form which was recognizably human.[21] We also learn that there are many other animal Group-souls, with all kinds of astral qualities. It is also the case that these

[19] For more about this topic, see my *Horoscope Handbook - a Rudolf Steiner Approach.*
[20] GA 99, lect. 25 May 1907.
[21] GA 105, Egyptian Myths and Mysteries, lect. 8.

four Group-souls are noble, benign beings, but as their 'projections' that is, the multitude of their animals, begin incarnating onto the Earth, they enter the field of influence exerted by Ahriman and Lucifer, and become somewhat degraded.[22] This degraded version of these Group-souls lives on in the human being, subtly active behind the outer show of human nature. For example, the negative feline qualities, or 'Lion forces', have an influence in the etheric body, especially of women, the negative bovine ('Bull forces') have an influence in the astral body, especially of men.

What is especially relevant to understanding the message of this second seal is, as Rudolf Steiner explained in his lecture cycle on the Apocalypse from 1908, that our current earthly personality or ego or "earthly I", has been developed from out of these primordial animal influences, but - importantly - this occurred, in conjunction with influences active in the soul, from the fourth influence, the 'potential human' Group-soul. This much higher influence has its origin in the Sun-sphere, where the cosmic Christ and beings who serve Him exist. This brings us to a contemplation of the nature of the 'Lamb of God' Group-soul.

The Christ-soul, symbolized by the Lamb, completes the four other Group-souls.
The structure of this sentence appears to be fragmented, and needs some clarification. It appears that what is meant is that the Lamb, representing the Group-soul of the spiritualized human beings, 'completes' or 'complements' the over-all **purpose** of the other Group-souls, in the sense that it provides the basis for a unified human life-wave of the future, formed of people who have overcome evil. This fifth Group-soul is new, in a sense. More precisely, it was formed in remote Ages, but as an Idea, a planned vessel, awaiting the redeemed human beings of the distant future to make it into an active reality.

The creating of this fifth Group-soul was a deed carried out by the cosmic Christ - the high sun-god Christ. As Rudolf Steiner revealed, the conditions necessary for this deed were prepared in the remote Sun aeon, when this great deity sacrificially undertook to limit its own evolving, its own evolutionary potential, and thus remain at a lesser rank of existence amongst the nine hierarchies, in order to stay nearer to the human life-wave. That Lazaros-John knew of this sacrificial decision, is shown by a passage in the Book of Revelation (13:8), where one sentence summarizes much of what we have been exploring,

> "All inhabitants of the earth will worship the Beast — all whose names have not been written in the Book of Life belonging to the Lamb, **who was slain from the creating of the world.**" (emphasis mine, AA)

This truth of the Lamb of God as the vessel providing an enveloping, sustaining, higher 'vessel' for redeemed humanity is also indicated in words of Christ Jesus, recorded by Lazaros-John in his Gospel (15:4),

> "Abide in me, and I in you. As the branch cannot bear fruit of itself, unless it abide in the vine, nor can you, unless you abide in me."

In my academic engagement with the mystical, esoteric texts of the Hellenistic Age from Judaic or Christian-Gnostic circles, I made a study of a little-known ancient Greek text which affirms this general idea of a future 'habitation' being prepared for humanity by Christ. The treatise is known as 4 Ezra; but the relevant section had not been correctly translated. Once its meaning was revealed by achieving a clearer

[22] When lesser animals 'incarnate', they are especially strongly subject to these malevolent influences.

translation, its message is very relevant to this second seal. Speaking here is the sun-god Christ,

> "For there was an occasion in the spiritual world, when for those human beings who now exist – before they were created – there was prepared by me, an Aion (spiritual realm) in which they may have abode (in the future)."[23] (trans. the author)

The Lamb of God and the 'Great Sacrifice'
At this point we need to contemplate further the 'Lamb of God' theme: this takes us into a deeply sacred theme concerning the sacrificial or selfless nature of the cosmic Christ. This means that we also need to explore the idea of the cosmic Christ becoming 'the new Group-soul for humanity'. Although Rudolf Steiner used the term 'Group-soul' in his revelations about the seal, and speaks of a "fifth Group-soul" to do with redeemed humanity, one feels that this term is not fully satisfactory. It certainly helps to clarify the meaning of the central image on the seal. But humanity of the future, when raised to the high level of consciousness implied here, will be primarily a 'spirit' rather than a soul; for we shall have developed by then the first member of our triune spirit nature, the Spiritual-self. In view of this, the term, 'Group-soul' can be understood as really referring to a 'Group-spirit'; but since such a thing did not exist in the past, Rudolf Steiner used the usual term for this new spiritual foundation of future humanity.

There is another kind of sacrifice which the sublime cosmic spirit has undertaken, to offer humanity a meaningful and joyous future. Rudolf Steiner refers to this as 'the Great Sacrifice'. He explained to an audience about a year after the Munich Conference, that the 'cosmic Christ', as the highest of the Powers or Spirits of Form, is actively undertaking the endeavour to advance up to the rank of the Dynameis, or 'Mights' as St. Paul calls these beings. And in doing this, indeed to actually achieve this, the cosmic Christ needs to, and also wills to, offer up his sublime spiritual nature (the equivalent of what we call our 'higher ego') in such a way as to provide the foundational element of spirituality for the human life-wave. This is what underlies the out-pouring of 'Grace' or deep spirituality to human souls; that is, if human beings gain a high spirituality, then the 'substance' of that spirituality has its origin in the offering of a sacred spiritual radiance from the divine "I" of Christ, to human souls.[24]

Rudolf Steiner's empowered initiatory clairvoyant consciousness enabled him to perceive this sacrificial act of the cosmic Christ, made in a previous Aeon. He was also able to perceive that the outcome for Him of this act shall be to arise, renewed, as one of the sublime Dynameis; this is the next level of divine beings above the Powers, in the cosmos.[25] Furthermore, Rudolf Steiner also provided some partially veiled indications about one process through which any human being who seeks spirituality becomes aligned to, or part of, the cosmic Christ light. His words actually point towards the activity of a great Archangel, known as 'Vidar' in the Edda. As I wrote, in my book about this Archangel: "in the final lecture of his lecture cycle on the Gospel of St. Luke, Rudolf Steiner begins to speak about something especially sacred, some mysterious

---

[23] The term I have translated as 'Aion' or spiritual world, (in Greek 'αἰών') to distinguish it from 'Aeon', the usually spelling, and meaning 'eternity'. But aeon as 'eternal Ages' here has no actual meaning. This same word as 'aeon' is used to mean a phase in the world's evolutionary history.

[24] This is also what is underlying the saving of the archetypal energy-structure of the human physical body.This very tenuous, invisible energy-body supports the material, flesh body.

[25] As taught in GA 102, lect. 24.3.1908.

soul quality which is also linked to the "finest forces of humanity". [26] He informed his audience that,

> As every person enters into incarnation, something is added to that person which does not arise from the process of conception, but which comes from the spiritual worlds....something is streamed into the person's ego, and it can be ennobled through the Christ impulse.
> This process is connected with the Mystery of Golgotha, because prior to that event, it did not happen. Thus every person has a "virgin birth"; something is given to him or her which is additional to that produced by the conception process and that which is so given, must be gradually developed and ennobled by assimilating the Christ impulse (*in life after life*).

Later in the lecture he adds,

> This new element can be gravely impaired if a person is entirely given over to materialistic thought. But it can be sublimated (*transformed and enriched*) if the person lets their nature be suffused by the warmth issuing from the Christ impulse, and then one can bring this into ever-higher forms in succeeding incarnations. People can destroy this additional element if they turn away from the Christ impulse, but they can nurture and develop it, if they receive into themselves what streams from the Christ Impulse.

At this point, we need to note these significant words from a different lecture cycle,

> We cannot gain awareness of the spirit through our own unaided activity towards spirituality; rather something has had to stream into our very being, from outside us, something which comes from the spiritual worlds, and which signifies a resurrection, a rejuvenation of us.[27]

We cannot go into the full mystery of the role of this Archangel Vidar in the redemption and renewal of the human being here, but in essence, Rudolf Steiner is indicating that from Christ Jesus, spiritual light which we can visualize as a kind of fountain from which the threefold human spirit derives, streams forth into the human soul. This is what transforms the human being, and brings that person into the Group-spirit called 'the Lamb of God'. It is this kind of self-sacrificing, self-surrendering, action which led to early initiates using the word 'lamb' as a title for Christ. The role of lambs in the human world has been that of a defenceless, creature who surrenders to the food or clothing needs of humans. But it is also the case that the term, 'Lamb of God' was used, because the events of Golgotha occurred when the sun was in the Age of Aries the Ram (747 BC - AD 1413).[28]

Another deep spiritual truth to contemplate when thinking of this seal, is that from the Dynameis or Mights, the Group-souls of the animals derive. These Group-souls were created in the Moon Aeon, by the Mights, as they rayed forth fields of astrality into the primordial predecessor of the Earth.
But the cosmic Christ, imbued as this high deity is, with the sublime Logos, and thereby also with the Father-God, shall be forming a Group-soul (or Group-spirit) of a much higher type than what the Mights have created. We note here that this divinity is

---

[26] The book is: *The Vidar Flame-Column: its meaning from Rudolf Steiner: from the Edda to Grail Christianity*.
[27] GA 129, *Wonders of the World, Ordeals of the Soul, Revelations of the Spirit*, lect. 25.Aug. 1911.
[28] In the year of the Golgotha events, AD 33, the sun was also in the constellation of Pisces, the Fishes, but that was not considered so relevant a fact when this the term was chosen, (see my *The Lost Zodiac of Rudolf Steiner* for detailed charts about this.

not the 'Logos Christ', who exists in the transcendent Trinity, who is the creator of the zodiac, but is the highest of the Powers. Finally, we need to note the reason that these three primary animal forms and also the potential human form arose in our cosmos in the course of its evolution, is that these derive from the zodiacal influences active in the four aeons. In the Saturn Aeon, Leo forces were predominant, in the Sun Aeon, Scorpio (eagle) forces were predominant, in the Moon Aeon, Aquarius forces were predominant; and in our current Aeon, Taurus influences are predominant; hence the very widespread reverence of the Pleiades and Taurus, amongst ancient peoples, who still had initiates guiding them.

The zodiacal time markers

Around the seal are 12 markers, which refer to the 12 zodiac influences; but four of these markers are different, they are ornamental, crown-like figures. These four symbols of nobility refer to the four cardinal zodiac influences that have been operative throughout humanity's evolution. These are Leo, Scorpio, Taurus and Aquarius. These four zodiacal influences are directly linked with the four aeons, and the four apocalyptic beings shown in the seal: Lion, Eagle, Bull and Human. They are also linked to the 'fourfold human being': the physical body, the etheric body, the astral body and the ego. Below is a brief summary of these interlinked connections. These inter-connections are not universal; they relate to the evolutionary process only. For instance, in our current existence the correlations are different. For example - leaving aside for a moment the evolutionary dynamics of the past - Leo forces are present in the feline species and humanity's etheric body; while bird species are related to our astral body and to Aquarian influences.

Aeon	**Zodiac sector**	**Human aspect**	**Creature type**
Saturn	Leo	Will and physical body (its non-material template)	Felines
Sun	Scorpio (its higher aspect: eagle)	Etheric body	Birds
Moon	Aquarius	Astral body	Human soul (as potential vessel of Spiritual-self)
Earth	Taurus	material body & earthly ego-sense	Bovines

It is very useful to contemplate the north blue window of the Goetheanum in this connection, as it deals with the same theme.[29] We also need to note that the seal, as painted for the Conference, appears to have an error in it as regards the positioning of the four cardinal signs. There should be two other signs between each of these four cardinal signs. But there is only one other sign between two of these cardinal markers, and yet between the other two cardinal markers there are three of these signs. This is spatially impossible, as regards both the signs and the constellations. I have concluded that this arrangement of the hour markers is due to a misunderstanding by the artist, and not a deliberate feature from Rudolf Steiner, because his original sketch is very imprecise. The four creatures are drawn in roughly, and not precisely aligned to their cardinal sign, and only some of the numerals are drawn in, and these are not precisely placed around the circle. It is this imprecise sequence which is depicted in the seal.

---

[29] See my *The Meaning of the Goetheanum Windows* for a comprehensive study of the scenes carved into them.

The group-souls or apocalyptic animals as stages in our evolution
As we have noted in Rudolf Steiner's explanations of the Apocalypse, the four apocalyptic creatures are primarily viewed as representing the evolutionary destiny of primordial humanity, as intertwined with that of the animal Group-souls. But in an early lecture on the Apocalypse, given in 1904, Rudolf Steiner indicated that we can contemplate the four apocalyptic creatures from an historical perspective; a view which considers the four creatures as representing recent cultural Ages, rather than animal related Group-souls. In fact, they can be seen as representing the first four Ages of the Post-Atlantean epoch. Furthermore, these cultural Ages then become seen as a recapitulation of earlier, large epochs. His words in the lecture were only briefly noted down, but below is the essence of what he taught in 1904,

The **Eagle** is representing the primal Indian Age (7227 - 5067 BC), and this Age also represents (i.e., recapitulates) qualities instilled during the Lemurian epoch.

The **Lion** is representing the primal Persian Age (5067-2907 BC), and this Age also represents qualities instilled during the Atlantean epoch.

The **Bull** is representing the ancient Egyptian-Mesopotamian Age (2907 - 747 BC), and this Age also represents qualities instilled during the Post-Atlantean epoch.

The (potential) **Human-being** is representing qualities instilled during the Greco-Latin Age (747 BC- AD 1413), and this Age also represents the next epoch; the future Manichaean Epoch. This epoch commences soon after AD 8000, and in this epoch the ego-hood from the Greco-Latin Age, in both its positive and negative aspects manifests strongly.

We can also note that from this perspective, although the fifth Group-soul was not a theme in the 1904 lecture, the Lamb would then represent the Epoch of the Seals, (or the Manichaean Age) wherein the Christ-impulse shall blossom in the ascending or spiritualizing branch of humanity. For Rudolf Steiner taught some years later, in lectures from 1909, that "those who have developed their spiritual potential, will be ready to receive 'Manas' - the Spiritual-self - in the 4th, 5th and 6th cultural Ages of this epoch of the Seals".[30] From other lectures on the Apocalypse, we learn that those human beings of the Epoch of the Seals who seek the spirit, shall achieve a high spiritual state, to the extent that the need for reincarnating ceases for them.

The 24 Elders: 'the journeying-past of the Elder Brothers...'
This enigmatic reference is about a helping, supervising, activity from higher beings, during humanity's evolution. Rudolf Steiner briefly indicated that unspecified, divine hierarchical beings assist humanity during each of the large cycles which make up every Aeon. There are 7 such cycles in every aeon; but we are only halfway through the fourth aeon, the 'Earth Aeon'. So we have gone through seven cycles in the Saturn, Sun and Moon Aeons (= 21 cycles) and, so far, 3 cycles only in this Earth Aeon (21 + 3 = 24 cycles). The beings who have been supervising our evolution in these 24 cycles are the "24 Elders". These great guiding beings were once described by him, in a lecture to priests, by using a Latin phrase, "existing within the realms of Eternity".[31] We end our contemplation of this seal by observing that the four 'apocalyptic creatures' are the basis of the ancient esoteric symbol, the Sphinx. That is the initiates in ancient times, especially in Mesopotamia (the Sumerians, etc) and in Egypt, perceived the same evolutionary processes as these seals depict, and created the sphinx image as a result.

---

[30] GA 104a lect. 21st May 1909.

[31] Lecture 8. Sept. 1924, the Latin phrase was *sub specie aeternitatis* which means, more literally, "within "the appearance (or aspect) of Eternity". But 'eternity' here really means 'in Devachan'.

SEAL THREE

The Four Horsemen

The drama of humanity's evolution through the cycles of time

What do we see?

Four horsemen on horses of different colours.

Ahead of these are three symbols representing spiritual qualities.

In the centre of the seal, a book which had been sealed or locked, but now its seven wax 'seals' have been broken open, allowing the book to be opened up.

Above this opened book are four oil-burning lamps.

At the top, seven trumpets, two of which are being blown by Angelic beings.

Rudolf Steiner's explanations tell us that this seal is about the different dynamics which arise and confront us human beings as crucial challenges, in our evolutionary history. How we meet these challenges in an earlier Age, determines the dynamics that we will manifest in a future Age.

It is very important to note that these four horsemen are representing not simply one evolutionary sequence of time, but five different sequences in our evolution.

For example, they can be considered from the viewpoint of a sequence of the four Aeons, the Saturn, Sun, Moon and Earth aeons, telling us what dynamics are occurring in these vast periods of evolution. But then, as a separate spiritual message, they can be contemplated as signifiers of a sequence of Epochs, such as Lemuria and Atlantis; or again, as signifiers of a sequence of Ages, such as the primal Indian, primal Persian and Greco-Latin cultural Ages, etc. This multi-layered quality inherent in the seal is due to the dynamics of smaller, later evolutionary cycles recapitulating the dynamics which manifested in earlier, larger ones.

Rudolf Steiner's explanation of Seal 3

A: Written report of the 1907 Munich Congress (GA 34, p. 598)

The Third Seal

The third seal represents the secrets of the so-called "Harmony of the Spheres". The human being experiences these secrets in the transitional time between death and new birth, in 'Spiritland' or in what is referred to normally in theosophical literature as 'Devachan'. However the representation provided in this seal is not actually this 'harmony' {*or music*} as experienced in Spiritland, but rather it alludes to the way that the dynamics of this realm are reflected into the astral realm. In regard to this, it must be firmly held in mind that all seven seals are experiences within the astral realm: it is also the case that other realms can be seen in the astral realm, in a reflected way. The Angels blowing trumpets in this image represent the primal spiritual Beings (*who are the creators*) of the manifested cosmos. (*That is, the higher hierarchical beings who, from Devachan, generated the 'Ideas' of all that exists in the physical world.*) The book with seven seals signifies that in the experiences which this seal portrays, the {*great*} riddle of existence is unveiled. The "Four Horsemen of the Apocalypse" represent humanity's evolution through long time-cycles of the Earth's evolution.

B: Conference lecture: 21st May 1907

The Third Seal

The third seal shows an opened book, surrounded by dish-shaped oil lamps and Angels blowing trumpets, enveloped in light and colours. The trumpeting Angels represent the Music of the Spheres. When one arises from the astral plane to Devachan, then one has the experience that the flowing light and colours of the astral plane are permeated by the Music of the Spheres. Then what one can see within the astral plane as flowing light and colours, begins to resonate with sound. This demonstrates that it is an expression of the nature of the Mental plane (*or Devachan*). The school of Pythagoras designated these harmonious sounds as 'the Music of the Spheres'. And Goethe speaks of this when he says in his play, *Faust*: "The Sun resounds as it did of old..."[32] and, "The new-born day is born, resounding to spirit ears!"[33]

The lamps represent the so-called 'vials of wrath'; this means, that the human being shall have attained to the spirit, and therefore will have overcome, or transformed, that which one calls 'fury'. All that which is of anger and fury must be cast out (*of the soul*) for this reason are the vials of wrath (*described as being*) poured out (*in Revelation*). The especial purpose of the book depicted inside the seal is, to indicate that the human being itself, in its evolution - once one understands how to correctly read its secrets - is a reflected image of the eternal evolution of the cosmos. If a person cognizes that the human being itself is an image of cosmic evolution, then that person can read himself; he or she has become a book.

C: Lecture of 16th September, 1907

The Third Seal

When we go far, far back into the course of humanity's evolving, so far that we look back over millions of years, then we experience something still different (*to what the second seal took us back to*). In our times, the human being is physically present on the

---

[32] From Faust, *Prologue in Heaven*: in the version of B. Taylor, "the sun-orb sings, in emulation 'mid brother spheres, his ancient round".

[33] From Faust, Part 2, Act 1: in the version of B. Taylor, "...Sounding loud to spirit-hearing, See the new-born day appearing !"

Earth, but there was once a time when that which traversed the Earth here and there (*i.e., the various living organisms*), was not able to be a suitable vessel for a human soul. The soul was therefore still on the astral plane; and we can go still further back, when the human soul existed on the spiritual level, in Devachan. In the future, the soul shall again ascend to this lofty stage, after the soul has been cleansed by (*lifetimes on*) the Earth. So, from the spiritual level, through the astral, and then to the physical plane and then again back up to the spiritual: that is the long evolutionary path of the human being.

And yet, all of this appears to be only of short duration, when you compare this to the evolutionary time involved in what humanity went through in the Saturn Aeon and the other aeons. In these remote aeons, the human being went through not only physical transformations, but also through spiritual and astral, as well as physical, transformations. And if one seeks to investigate these transformations, and follow them in vision, then one has to, (*as a seer*), ascend up into the higher realms. There one hears the Music of the Spheres: tones which flow through the space (*i.e., the environment around one*). And if the human being is to again live into this spiritual realm, then the Music of the Spheres will resound to him or her. This experience is called in esotericism, 'the trumpet-calls of the Angels'.

For this reason, this third seal includes the trumpets. From the spiritual world come the revelations, but these only reveal their actual meaning to that person, when he or she has advanced further along the path. At that point, the book its seven wax seals opened out, is then made manifest to the student; the wax seals now disclose their meaning to the student. It is actually these opened wax seals which we see spread out around the now open book.[34] It is because of this process, that the book is placed in the centre of the image, whilst below there are depicted four primary phases of humanity's evolution. For the four horse riders are actually the developmental phases which humanity has to go through.

D: From the brief comments in the October Folio

...from the astral realm the archetypes of our physical world can be observed; and the after-images of the Spiritual world (Devachan) can be seen in the astral realm. Accordingly, seal three portrays the astral after-images of 'Spiritland' (Devachan). The Angels who are blowing trumpets represent the primordial spiritual beings behind the cosmos with all of its manifestations. The trumpet blasts themselves represent the energies which ray forth from these beings into the world, and through which the various beings and objects in the world are crafted and sustained in their evolving and their activity.

The apocalyptic riders represent the main evolutionary phases which a human individual journeys through, in the course of many incarnations and which are portrayed in the astral realm as riders on four horses. A glowing white horse: depicting a very early stage of the soul's evolution. A fire-coloured horse: signifying the warring phase of humanity's evolution. Then a black horse, corresponding to that soul-stage where only the external, physical perception of the soul has developed. And finally a green-shimmering horse - the image of the spiritually matured soul who has gained mastery over the body. For this reason it has the green shade of colour, which arises as the expression of the life-forces, when these are exerting an influence out into the world, from within the human being.

---

[34] Rudolf Steiner taught in his 1908 and 1909 lectures on the Apocalypse (GA 104, 104a) that the opening of these 7 wax seals, signifies that the dynamics of the 7 Cultural Ages in the future 6th Large Epoch (the Manichean Epoch) are seen by the initiate.

COMMENTARY: SEAL THREE

The 3 geometrical forms

The Pentagram: is a symbol for the Spiritual-self

The Hexagram: is a symbol of the Life-spirit

The Heptagram: it appears that this symbol was only referred to by Rudolf Steiner on one or two occasions only, where he explains that it symbolizes the leading spiritual power of the solar system, that is, the cosmic Christ. One would expect that here in this seal that it represents the Spirit-human, the highest of the triune human spiritual, but this is uncertain. It may be that it symbolizes here not quite the Spirit-human, but a stronger alignment to the Christ-light than the two lower spirit aspects: a kind of preliminary stage towards the Atma or Spirit-human.

So, from the spiritual level, through the astral, and then the physical plane (on p.37) This appears to be a reference to the 'Phases' of a 'Cycle' of evolution in our Earth Aeon. The diagram in Appendix One shows how each cycle in evolution has seven phases in it; so then Rudolf Steiner's remarks here, which are only brief general comments, refer to the first four phases of the fourth cycle of our Earth Aeon. The first phases occur within Devachan, then our solar system steps down into the astral level in phase 3, and then in the fourth phase, evolution enters into the material, physical level (the black horse). Then after that, this dynamic is reversed, and the solar system proceeds up into the spiritual realms, (see next section about the 4 Horsemen).

The Four Horsemen

In the Book of Revelation, these Four Horsemen are omens of torments to come; they bring great suffering upon the Earth, and Rudolf Steiner reveals that in terms of the Book of Revelation, they refer primarily to the future Epoch of the Seals, or the Manichaean Epoch. But in this seal, they represent the journey through past evolutionary Ages of humanity. This is not inconsistent with the meaning of the imagery in Revelation itself, as the imagery and the general story line in this deeply esoteric Biblical text has several layers of meaning. There are several interpretations given to these horsemen in the various lectures given by Rudolf Steiner on this topic. Most are about the past evolutionary journey of humanity, but one of the meanings is about our future.

The Meaning of The Four Horsemen

Viewpoint 1:
From the perspective of a vast over-view of our evolution: the 4 aeons
One meaning of these four figures is connected to a very large over-view of human evolution: the four aeons. The indications about this perspective are only briefly recorded in the lecture of 16th September 1907:

> "….. And yet each of these appears to be quite short, when you compare this to the evolutionary time involved in what humanity went through in the Saturn (*aeon*) and the other aeons. In these remote aeons, the human being went through not only physical, transformations, but also through spiritual and astral, as well as physical transformations." (p. 39)

Contemplating the seal from this viewpoint, we visualize:
This meaning of the four riders is based on a very long-term perspective of human evolution. One then sees the four riders as representing the four aeons through which we have developed the physical, etheric and astral bodies, then the ego-sense. Then the three geometrical forms represent the following three aeons in which we develop the Spiritual-self, Life-spirit and the Spirit-human, respectively.

White Horse: the Saturn aeon, where humanity was in a condition not yet darkened by any earthly, material influences.

Red Horse: the Sun aeon, where humanity existed in a radiant sun-illumined sphere, permeated with fiery warmth, but there are now negative ('fallen') beings.

Black Horse: the Moon aeon, where humanity received its initial, very primitive, dark, lowly animalistic astral body.

Pale Horse: the current Earth aeon, where in the solid, earthly environment, the sense of ego develops.

Therefore the opened book, with its seven seals unsealed, here represents the 7 aeons. Consequently, the 4th opened book-seal is depicting the crucial, pivotal 4th aeon. Upon the successful development of the ego-sense in this 4th aeon, depends the outcome of the remaining 3 aeons, wherein the threefold human spirit should be developed. This also implies that the sense of "I" when gained in this aeon, will not stay at a somewhat illusory personal level, with the potential danger of a hardened egoistic self, which invokes a lower, malignant astral nature. The gods are striving to ensure that for as many people, as possible the Earth Aeon results in an ego-sense which in a preliminary sense, develops some of the qualities of the higher "I" or higher-self.

Viewpoint 2:
From the perspective of an over-view of the descending and ascending Phases of the 4th Cycle of the Earth aeon
From the brief notes made from Rudolf Steiner's lecture on 16th September, 1907, we can also see that there is another meaning of these four figures, which is based a long-term view of evolution, but not as vast as in the first perspective. His explanation is very brief, and this perspective is about a broad general view only,

> "So, from the spiritual level, through the astral, and then the physical plane and then again back up the spiritual: that is the long evolutionary path of the human being...but not as long as the path involving the Saturn Aeon (*and other Aeons*) ...." (p. 41)

It involves a descending down from the Devachanic level to the astral level, then to the earthly and then back up again. This correlates to the first four phases of the fourth cycle of our aeon, see Diagram 1. Since Rudolf Steiner's words about this were only briefly noted down, we can have only a less detailed, more general view of how to correlate the horsemen in this correlation, to the past evolution of humanity.

White Horse: humanity was on a Devachanic level (Phases 1 & 2 of the 4th Cycle)

Red Horse: humanity descended to the astral level (Phase 3 of the 4th Cycle)

Black Horse: humanity descends down to the material level (our current situation: Phase 4 of the 4th Cycle)

Pale Horse: humanity will return to a spiritual level (in Phases 5, 6, 7 of the 4th Cycle)

For a comprehensive diagram explaining the complex array of Cycles, Phases and Epochs through which we have been taken through during our evolutionary path, see my *Rudolf Steiner Handbook.*

Viewpoint 3:
A message about the large Epochs in our current Phase of the Earth aeon
This viewpoint, and the following one (viewpoint 4), are based on other lectures from Rudolf Steiner about Revelation; especially from May 15th 1909, in his cycle, *The Apocalypse of St. John*, from Oslo, (GA 104a). This gives us a much more detailed understanding of the horsemen.

Contemplating the seal from viewpoint 3, we visualize:

White Horse: the **Polarian** epoch: when humanity is in a very tenuous, innocent state. Ego-hood has not arisen, for humanity is still immersed in the vast spiritual-etheric energies of the gods, that is divine beings who exist on the spiritual level of the solar system. There is no solid material Earth, it is within the central sun-body; human consciousness is only a vague awareness of the physical or spiritual environs.

Red Horse: **Hyperborean** epoch: during this epoch, the Earth with its ethereal, tenuous primordial human beings, is cast out of the Sun. Humanity now has to do battle with an increasingly alien environment, as the planet begins to become firstly a warm gaseous world which is constantly changing. Then, as the planet condenses further, a denser element, a misty vaporous watery element, appears for the first time. (This epoch correlates to the creation of the Kant-Laplace nebula formation, in terms of astronomical cosmogony.)

Black Horse: **Lemurian** epoch: in this epoch, as the Earth becomes denser, its watery gaseous environment becomes more viscous, and a fiery volcanic quality appears. As it becomes ever denser, mineralized substances appear, and the human body also becomes denser. After the extrusion of the Moon, and human beings start to incarnate, their consciousness gradually becomes restricted to the physical, material world.

During this epoch the state of soul arises wherein human beings perceive only the outer external material world.

Pale Horse: **Atlantean** epoch: in this epoch, (ending about 7,500 BC) the primary development for humanity consisted of the forming of the frontal lobe of the brain. This enabled the first glimmers of an ego-sense, and also provided the basis for an earthly intelligence: the intellectual capacity. The astral body was beginning to achieve the capacity, through its influence in the etheric body, to have some power over the formative processes in its physical body.

Now, from this viewpoint, this pale horse is depicting the crucial, pivotal 4th epoch; the Atlantean epoch. In this 4th epoch, more impulses towards a true human soul-state become active, from divine beings in the sun-sphere, enabling at least a preliminary spirituality to develop, so that the lower, animalistic tendencies are reduced in their power over the human being. Many human beings in the Atlantean epoch had actual animal traits in their face, especially that of the bovine or feline or avian animals To the degree that the Atlantean folk reduced those animal qualities during that epoch, this would assist some spiritual impulses to arise during the remaining 3 epochs, in which the threefold human spirit should develop in a rudimentary way.

These are the epochs which occur after Atlantis; the first is the one in which we are now living, called the Post-Atlantean Epoch; then comes the Manichaean Epoch, and then a seventh, un-named, epoch. One of the ways that the cultural-religious leaders in Atlantis, the initiates, sought to help their people in this challenge of developing some higher astrality, was to create temples which were substantially formed from many statues, that is, many carved busts of the people; these statues depicted how a person looked in an earlier life.[35] The spiritual seekers of that epoch (the acolytes in the Mystery Centres) had an awareness of a journey that they were engaged in over lifetimes, a journey which had huge consequences for their own future, depending on how well or poorly they engaged with their spiritual tasks.

(Teachings about these epochs are in the book *Esoteric Science, an Outline* and in many lectures; in addition, my *Rudolf Steiner Handbook* gives an over-view of these epochs, together with diagrams.)

Viewpoint 4:
A message about the cultural Ages of the current epoch (the Post-Atlantean epoch)

Another valuable perspective for contemplating the horse-riders is given in Rudolf Steiner's lectures on Revelation from 1908 (GA 104) and 1909 (GA 104a). This perspective on humanity's evolution is a shorter-term historical view and involves the current Post-Atlantean large Epoch, in particular, the first four of its cultural Ages.
Contemplating the seal from viewpoint 4, we visualize:

The **WHITE** Horse is the **Primal Indian** cultural Age: This Age (7227-5067 BC) was a recapitulation of the Polarian Epoch. In this age, manifesting amongst people in ancient northern India, there was an unequalled natural awareness of the spiritual worlds, including Devachan. Led by the Rishis, an other-worldly feeling of existing within the One Divine Being was culturally widespread, and was actively sought for by acolytes on the path to higher wisdom; this is now known as the Vedanta wisdom. In the Book of Revelation, the letter to the church at Ephesos incorporates indications about these

[35] Archive document, 16.6.1904

dynamics. (This is because on a deeper level, as Rudolf Steiner reveals, the letter is referring to the Time-spirit or guiding spirit-being of the Primal Indian Age).[36]

The **RED** Horse is the **Primal Persian** cultural Age: This Age (5067-2907 BC) was a recapitulation of the Hyperborean Epoch. In this age, manifesting amongst people in ancient Persia, people began to struggle with the fact of evil; the battle between Light and Darkness became a major theme in their religious-cultural life. This was an ancient forerunner to the historical Zarathustrian religion; it arose from a very early incarnation of Zarathustra in this epoch. In this Age, the fighting, martial condition of the soul is predominant. This Age ended in a terrible war with the ancient Turanian peoples, a war which literally lasted for centuries.[37] (In the Book of Revelation, the letter to the 'church' at Smyrna incorporates indications about these dynamics.)

The **BLACK** Horse is the **Egyptian-Mesopotamian** cultural Age: This Age (2907-747 BC) was a recapitulation of the Lemurian Epoch. Ahrimanic influences increase, despite the persistence of high and noble Mystery Centres, the most significant of which, such as the Great Pyramid, were established about 2,900-2,700 BC. There is a focus on developing sacred places in accordance with mathematical-geometrical motions of the heavenly bodies. But also a subtle materialism emerges towards the end of this age and a decadent occultism develops.

The **PALE** Horse (the colour of this horse in Revelation (6:8) is a pale greenish yellow, (in Greek, chloros - χλωρός.)
This horse is the **Greco-Latin** Age: This Age (747 BC - AD 1413) was a recapitulation of the Atlantean Epoch. The Atlanteans were people who began to experience mental images (also called, 'ideation'), whereas the ancient Greeks were people who by now could progress from just mental images, up to the forming of real concepts, to substantial intellectual thinking.[38]

The primary soul development achieved in this Age was a stronger sense of ego-hood, as manifested through the intellect. An intellectual, logical capacity develops for the first time, yet with this there came an abstract intellectuality. But in addition, an exceptional level of artistic skill in painting and sculpture, and this combined with acute sensory awareness, led to great architectural achievements, bringing much beauty to these cultures. The subtle feeling for the influence of the etheric energies in the physical body and in nature was a significant factor in the achievements of the Greeks, both in the arts and in sport (the Olympic Games). In this connection Rudolf Steiner mentions that the greenish colour indicates the ethers exerting an active power in human life generally.

The 4th horse is depicting the crucial, pivotal 4th cultural Age, the Greco-Latin Age. It was in this Age that the Mystery of Golgotha occurred, an event which brought about an infusion of the Earth's aura with the majestic sun-spirit, Christ. The outcome of the three remaining Ages depends very substantially on the development of an ego-sense in this 4th Age. For the 5th Age, that is, our current Age (AD 1413-3573) is to assist the spiritual-soul faculty (or intuitive consciousness) to develop.

---

[36] I prefer the spelling 'Ephesos' instead of the customary 'Ephesus', because the latter is a Latinized version of the Greek name.

[37] GA 123, lect.1st Sept.1910

[38] Rudolf Steiner, briefly noted in a lecture of 16.6.1904.

The 6th Age is to encourage the Spiritual-self faculty to develop, at least in an initial sense. The 7th Age is to bring to a satisfactory completion what the earlier Ages have made possible, perhaps even a small beginning of the Life-spirit as well. But such is the intensity and dangers and struggles caused now by earthly sense of self, that for many people, the 7th Age shall bring about a hardened ego-ism in their soul, leading finally to the great War of All against All.

Regarding this catastrophic event at the end of the 7th Age, Rudolf Steiner taught that the ascending, that is spiritualizing, human beings will not be harmed in that time; either because most shall not be incarnate then, or those small numbers who are, shall be spiritually protected. It was with these momentous revelations in mind that he told his audience in Norway that in absorbing anthroposophical truths, the soul is absorbing the Christ-reality. This immense statement needs an entire book, but we can note here that the *intellectual* absorption only of anthroposophical truths is not what he is referring to. For these high concepts must then permeate the heart, causing a profound impetus towards a purity and compassion in the feelings, and a sense of the sacred as a reality, otherwise an intensified egoism can result.

Viewpoint 5:
Contemplating the 4 horsemen as signifying our distant future:
We can see that the above shorter-term evolutionary perspective, viewpoint 4, reveals a very significant fact. The core spiritual dynamics of earlier large epochs are recapitulated in the Post-Atlantean cultural Ages. But Rudolf Steiner goes further, and points out that the core spiritual dynamics of the epochs and their related Ages shall re-emerge in the far future: in the next large Epoch, known as the Manichaean Epoch, which will commence shortly after AD 8000. In contemplating the seal we can now focus on a hidden reference to humanity's future. So this is another perspective we can take up when contemplating the seal. Again it is in his primary lecture cycles on the Apocalypse, from 1908 and 1909 that these indications are found.

Contemplating the seal from viewpoint 5, we visualize:

The Manichaean Epoch
We noted earlier that one perspective alluded to in the seal is about our future. In particular it is about the kind of dynamics that will be significant in the first four cultural ages of the large 'Manichaean epoch'. This epoch commences after the War of All against All, so it is due to start shortly after AD 8,000.

The 1st age: The White horse indicates the main qualities developed in the primal Indian Age, and the extent to which that spirituality has been enhanced in all lifetimes since then, for this shall be dynamically empowering our spiritual consciousness.

The 2nd age: The Red horse indicates the main qualities developed in the primal Persian Age, and the extent to which that spirituality has been enhanced since then, for this will become an influence which directly enhances our spirituality.

The 3rd age: The Black horse indicates that the highest qualities incorporated into the soul during the Egypto-Mesopotamian Age shall become a primary influence ennobling the soul during our lives in this future Age.

The 4th age: The Pale horse indicates that the finest qualities developed in the Greco-Latin Age, and the extent to which that spirituality has been enhanced in all lifetimes since then, will become a force dynamically uplifting the human soul.

The reflecting of dynamics into a later age
Below is a list which integrates all of the positive meanings of the four horse-riders, in terms of the epochs and their corresponding cultural Ages. You can read these downwards, and also across the page. This recapitulating or reflecting of, the dynamics from the Epochs into the Cultural Ages is explained in the main lecture cycle of 1909 in Oslo, and also in an archive document, a lecture from 10th October 1904.

WHITE Horse: Polaria - Primal Indian Age Ephesos (Manichaean cultural Age 1)

RED Horse: Hyperborea - Primal Persian Age Smyrna (Manichaean cultural Age 2)

BLACK Horse: Lemuria - Egypto-Mesopot. Age Pergamon (Manichaean cultural Age 3)

PALE Horse: Atlantis - Greco-Latin Age Thyatira (Manichaean cultural Age 4)

The larger periods (aeons, cycles) are too huge to be incorporated in this sequence.

The four burning lamps
In the Book of Revelation, the horse-riders are omens of terrible punishments to be inflicted on humanity - on the fallen or depraved branch of future humanity. But in the seal, this is not the case, as we have seen. Rudolf Steiner indicated that instead, it is the burning lamps which are signifying such omens of future ordeals. So, the above exploration of the uplifting, ennobling spiritual influences which shall be operative in the Manichaean epoch, presents the future dynamics for the good, the Christ-aligned, human beings. But elsewhere on the planet, the fallen branch of humanity shall be undergoing the ordeals represented by the lamps.

The Trumpets
Although in the Book of Revelation the trumpets signify the events and dynamics that shall manifest in the 7th large epoch - the epoch after the Manichaean epoch - this is not what they signify in this seal. Here they represent the influences from the high realm of Devachan, raying into what is an astral image. This in turn implies that, if with astral clairvoyance the acolyte sees this seal in the astral realm, or gets some visual psychic imagery associated with the seal, then it is possible for that person who does not actually have a clairvoyance or higher consciousness which reaches up to Devachan, to also experience some higher insights, from Devachan. Such insights are usually a subtle 'whispering', subtle 'awarenesses', which are perceived as if being inwardly heard.

Note: the Pale Horse Rider
It is quite clear that Clara Rettich has painted the rider on this pale horse as if this rider is only just seated on the horse. The body language of the imagery here is, that the human being has a somewhat disengaged, tenuous participation. The rider is scarcely gripping the horse - holding onto the mane, for there is no bridle. And the rider is seated far too far back, almost sliding off the horse. (It is also possible that the rider here is a feminine figure.)

However, an examination of Rudolf Steiner's sketch reveals that he did not draw the rider in this position, or any precise position, because all four riders are only very roughly sketched. So it is very likely that in a private conversation he instructed Ms. Rettich to depict the pale horse rider in this way. That this unusual body language of the rider on the pale horse is the result of Rudolf Steiner's instructions to the artist, is supported by the fact that he asked Ms. Rettich to create these seals again, this time for the Stuttgart Centre. He would be unlikely to ask her to repeat her work for such a prominent and important setting, if she added striking details to any of the seals, for which he did not give permission.

It is always the fourth step in an evolutionary sequence, (the 4th Aeon, 4th Cycle, 4th Phase, etc) which is the pivotal crucial step. It is this fourth step which, on the basis of what was achieved in the first 3 steps, should enable the evolutionary momentum to move up to a new higher level, in the 5th, 6th and 7th steps.

Interpreting the Pale Horse Rider

What would a weak grasp by the rider of the horse, and the gesture of 'rising above' or 'moving away from' this horse mean, for the various viewpoints of the four horsemen?

Viewpoint 1: An over-view of evolution, the 4 aeons:

That the rider of the 4th horse is about to leave that horse means: humanity is pre-determined to ascend, through the portal of ego-hood, which the 4th aeon bestows, up to the higher consciousness states.

Viewpoint 2: Earth aeon over-view: the descending and ascending Phases of the 4th Cycle:

That the rider of the 4th horse is about to leave that horse means here: the 'cosmic tide' shall ensure that in the next Phases of the Earth's evolving, human beings ascend in their consciousness capacity from manifesting in the material plane, up to manifesting in higher realms.

Viewpoint 3: The large Epochs in our current Phase of the Earth aeon:

In this viewpoint, the rider of the 4th horse is about to leave that horse because: the 4th Epoch is that of Atlantis, and during this epoch, as Rudolf Steiner taught, that the horse species was created, and it was their existence, their impact on the elemental energies of the Earth-soul, which enabled modifications in the human brain structure to occur, enabling human beings to lay the foundations for a personal intelligence, thus rising above their primitive sentiency. This is the reason for the deep feeling that people often have about horses, a feeling that they somehow symbolize 'freedom'. The freedom on a deeper level is the capacity to experience one's own thoughts.

Viewpoint 4: The cultural Ages of the current epoch (the Post-Atlantean Epoch):

The rider of the 4th horse is about to leave that horse because: now, in the Greco-Latin Age, humanity will be enhancing their consciousness, thereby achieving a personal ego-sense. This occurs through the emergence of an individual analytical intelligence, hence the birth of logic and intellectual pursuits occur in this Age. This process is itself a result of recapitulating the Atlantean Age, wherein the physiological basis of a personal intelligence was laid down.

SEAL FOUR

The two columns: Jachin & Boaz

Reversing the soul's descent into matter

What do we see ?

Two columns stand before us, one on the sea, and the other on firm ground.

Each column has a letter on it, indicating that it is related to the 'Jachin' or 'Boaz' columns of Solomon's temple, which were taken up into Freemasonry and are a part of every lodge.

Above these is a cloud, in the midst of which is an opened book, held by two hands.

Above this is a radiant sun, with a face in it; signifying human beings whose existence is no longer in matter, but now far above the physical world, in the 'spiritual-sun'.

Again the rainbow is here, but this time arching around, enveloping the features in the upper part of the seal. The rainbow signifies the seven planetary energies, now purified.

Three symbols are placed in the black border area: the pentagram (the Spiritual-self), the hexagram (the Life-spirit) and also the symbol for the Sun.

This seal has much to say about how the human being can be reversing the descent into material consciousness, and encounter the polarity between the contemplative life and the active life.

The Philosopher's Stone

Rudolf Steiner's commentary on this seal, and seal seven, refers to "the Philosopher's Stone"; this is a term which first occurs in alchemical writings from about AD 300 (by an alchemist named Zosimos); but this term became much more widely known when it became prominent in Medieval alchemical texts. There it is indicated that this 'stone' is the elixir of life, able to transmute base metals into noble metals; it also gave immortality to those who discovered it. It has various meanings in these texts; including that of a powder which could actually transmute base metal into gold. But it is the spiritual meaning of the Philosopher's Stone which is the focus of Rudolf Steiner's comment on these seals. He indicates briefly that a common substance, carbon, when inwardly vivified by the powers of the etheric body, if these are enhanced by meditative exercises, plays a role in rejuvenating the physical body, displacing the dense substances of the physical body.

J
B

Rudolf Steiner's explanation of Seal 4

A: Written report of the 1907 Munich Congress (GA 34, p. 598)

Amongst other features, the fourth seal depicts two columns, one of which is placed on the sea, the other is set on solid land. In these columns the secret is alluded to of the role which the red (*oxygen-rich*) blood and the bluish-red (*carbon dioxide-rich*) blood have in humanity's evolution, and how this blood, in accordance with humanity's evolution, shall transform in the far future from its current condition, which it has had from ancient times. The letters on these columns point to this secret in a manner known only to the initiate. All explanations of both letters, given either in public writings, or in secret societies (*i.e. closed esoteric groups*), stay only at a superficial level.

The book in the clouds refers to a future condition of humanity, a condition in which all of humanity's knowledge shall have become internalized. In the *Revelation of St. John*, one finds these significant words about this: "I took a small book from the hand of the Angel, and swallowed it..."(10:10)

The sun in this image refers to a cosmic process, which shall happen simultaneously with that future evolutionary condition of humanity just referred to (*that is, wherein knowledge becomes internalized*). Then, the Earth shall be in an entirely different relation to the sun, and also to the condition of interrelatedness (*of the planets in the solar system*) which holds sway in the cosmos, in the current age. And in this seal, everything is so presented, that the arrangement of all the separate features, all the individual parts of it, correspond exactly to definite, actual processes (*involving humanity's significance in the solar system*).

B: Conference lecture: 21st May 1907

The Fourth Seal

The two columns in the fourth seal represent the 'blood-tree' composed of intertwining red and blue streams, (*existing in the human being*). The cloud is the present-day air, the only element over which the throat prevails. From out of this 'tree' there shall arise the generative power of the human being; a power which can exert its influence into dense matter. Above both of these columns, the initiated human being is coming into being: (*depicted here as*) that person who has swallowed the book. Then the human being produces in itself the power to transform the Earth into the Sun. When human beings attain to this stage, they shall have a capacity for spiritual cognizing, that is for seeing into the astral realm. This stage is indicated by the rainbow arching over the Sun. This rainbow depicts the power which the human being shall have made its own, when humans become beings who are cosmically creative.

> **Note**: at the beginning of the lecture, prior to discussing even the first seal, Rudolf Steiner spoke in some detail about the meaning of two large columns which were set up in the hall. These columns are somewhat similar to the columns which feature in Masonic lodges, they are also closely related to the columns depicted in the seal. Rudolf Steiner's comments about the large columns are given at the end of this section about the fourth seal.

C: Lecture, 16th September 1907

The Fourth Seal

There is an even higher stage of future evolution for us than what the third seal indicates. The human being derives from higher worlds and the human being shall ascend into these higher worlds (*in the future, as a permanent state of being*). Then the human form, in which we now exist, shall have disappeared. What is today outside in the world – (*the many different realms of nature, and its associated elemental energies, these are in effect*) the separate 'letters' (*of the Cosmic Word*) of which the human being is composed. All this the human being shall have taken up again into itself. By then the human being's form will have become identified with the form of the cosmos.

In a somewhat trivial presentation of Theosophy, one teaches and speaks about the idea that the human being 'should seek God in himself or herself'. But whoever wants to find God, must seek Him in His works, which are spread out in the cosmos. Nothing in the world consists entirely only of matter – that is illusory – in reality, all matter is an expression of spiritual reality; a herald of the active influences of God. And the human being shall, in future times, expand the limits of his nature. Humanity shall ever more identify with the form of the cosmos (*that is, become an expression of the cosmos in regard to our over-all form*). In this situation, one can then portray the human being in the form of the cosmos, instead of (*the current bodily*) human shape. You can see this in the fourth seal, with the rocks, the sea and the columns. That which today is to be seen everywhere in the world as clouds, this shall provide from its substance, that which will form the human body.

> **Note:** That is, the etheric energies of the Earth, of which clouds are a direct condensation, shall be the basis of the future etherealized body.

The energies which are today (*an integral part of*) the (*consciousness of the*) Spirits of the Sun, shall in the future, provide that which will become the human being's intellectual-spiritual qualities, but on an infinitely higher level than our intelligence of today. It is this faculty of the spiritual Sun[39] (*towards which the human being is striving*).

In contrast to the plants which have their 'head', that is, their roots, inclined towards the centre of the Earth, the human being directs its head towards the Sun: and the human being shall (*in the future*) unite with the Sun and receive higher forces from it. This is portrayed in the sun-countenance which has its basis on the cloud-body, the rocks and the columns. The human being shall then have Creator powers within itself and as a symbol of the perfected (*fully spiritualized*) Creation, the human being is surrounded by the coloured rainbow. A similar image can be found in Revelation (10:1). In the middle of the cloud is a book. In the Apocalypse it is said that the initiate has to swallow the book. In this way, the future Age is indicated in which the human being does not only receive wisdom from outside itself, but exists in a condition wherein the soul will be nourished by wisdom, just as today we become permeated by the food we eat. It shall be an Age in which the human being will be an embodiment of wisdom.

D: From the brief comments in the October Folio

The fourth Seal....In these columns the secret is brought to expression which is signified by the role which the red blood and the bluish-red blood have, in human evolution. The human "I" undergoes its development in the course of earthly existence,

---

[39] Spiritual Sun: the German text is literally, *"Sonnenkraft"* i.e., (spiritual) 'solar power'.

by bringing its life physically to expression in the reciprocal activity between red blood, without which the human being has no life, and the bluish blood, without which the human being has no cognizing. Blue blood is the physical manifestation of energies which bestow cognizing, *(and hence knowledge)*. But it is this blood stream which, in the human form, is itself responsible for death. Whereas in the human form, the red blood stream is the manifestation of life, but this stream by itself cannot bestow any capacity for cognizing.

These two blood-streams, in their reciprocal interaction, portray the Tree of Knowledge (*of Good and Evil*) and the Tree of Life; or one could also say, they represent the two columns, on the basis of which, both life **and** the cognitional ability of the "I", (*through which knowledge is gained*), continue to develop, until that degree of perfection is attained wherein the human being becomes one with the universal terrestrial forces. (*That is, with planetary and zodiacal energies which permeate and actively influence humanity in this earthly world.*) This attainment is depicted on the seal by the upper part (*of the human*) body which consists of clouds, and also through the countenance which has taken into itself the forces of the Sun. Then the cognizing (*of wisdom*) that the human being experiences, shall no longer be received from outside itself, for this shall have been 'swallowed' into itself; this is signified by the book in the centre of the seal. It is only on the basis of this swallowing (*i.e., absorbing into oneself of wisdom*) when we are living on a higher level of existence, that the seven seals of the book can open up; as is already indicated in seal three. In the Book of Revelation, one finds these significant words (*about this situation*): "And I took the little book from the hand of the Angel and swallowed it…" (10:10)

The two columns (lecture, 21st May, 1907)

> **Note:** Rudolf Steiner's words so far, were about the two columns which are depicted in the fourth seal. But two large columns, with the initials J and B, standing for Jachin and Boaz, were also placed in the hall for the Conference. These are similar to the two columns in the seal, and to the prominent pillars or columns which every Freemason temple or Lodge has. The general explanation of their meaning in Masonry is simply that they represent the strength and stability of Freemasonry, and are symbolic of the power of God in his Creation. But Rudolf Steiner explains that they are more than that.

What do these two columns signify in Rosicrucianism? If one seeks to explain these two columns which we have before us, one has to start with (*a legendary account now known as the 'Temple Legend', recorded in the 12th century book called*) 'the Golden Legend'.[40]

This says:

"When Seth, the son of Adam – he who had stepped forward in the place of Abel – had attained the required (*soul*) development, he was permitted to gain a glimpse of Paradise. Seth was permitted to pass by the fiery Angel who holds a sword, and enter into the sacred site from which the (*primordial*) human being (*the fallen Adam*) had been driven out. There Seth beheld something quite remarkable. He saw how the two

[40] Rudolf Steiner now narrates a legend about Seth and the Tree of Life in Paradise, found in the collection of stories about saints and semi-mythical Christian themes, called "The Golden Legend", written by Jacques de Voragine in the 13th century. But he narrates a Freemasonry-oriented variant of the legend.

trees, the Tree of Life and the Tree of Knowledge of Good and Evil, were intertwined. Seth received three seeds from these two intertwined trees; he took these seeds and placed them in the mouth of his deceased father, Adam. Then there grew from the grave of Adam a mighty tree. This tree was revealed, to those with spiritual perceiving, as raying forth a mighty, fiery radiance. For those with the capacity for spiritual perception, this fiery radiance drew itself together, to form the letters, J and B."

(Rudolf Steiner inserts here a personal remark about the Freemasonry aspect:)

These are the first letters of two words, the speaking forth of which (*here*) I am not permitted, by spiritual powers. But the meaning of these words is: I am who I was, I am who now is, I am who shall be.

Note: The German text of his personal remarks here appears to be defective. Rudolf Steiner apparently is telling his audience that he is not permitted to pronounce or speak forth, the words "Jachin" and "Boaz": see the Commentary where this defective sentence is discussed.

(Rudolf Steiner continues with the legend)
"This tree separated into three parts. Seth took wood from it, and this wood has been used since then in many ways, during the later evolving of humanity and the world. The legend tells that a staff was made from it: the staff of Moses. And it was from the same wood that beams in Solomon's temple were carved. These beams remained there for as long as humanity retained understanding of the old secrets. Then the wood was cast into a lake, from whose waters, in a particular point of time, the blind and the lame were healed. After that, the wood was retrieved and made into the bridge across which the Saviour walked, on His way to the cross. The cross itself, upon which the Saviour hung, was made from the wood which had grown out of the mouth of Adam, after the seeds from the intertwined trees of Life and of Knowledge had been placed in his mouth."

This then is the legend (*about the Tree of Life*), which has deep symbolic meaning. Recall now that process, that transformation, of which the spiritual student has to be aware, when he or she undergoes the fourth stage of the Rosicrucian path of spiritual development: the producing (*in oneself*) of the Philosopher's Stone. We remind ourselves now that this producing of the Philosopher's Stone involves a certain way of inwardly working with the red blood stream. We can think about the significance of this red blood, not only because in the Goethean statement we are taught; "Blood is a very special fluid", but because esoteric knowledge of all ages has also taught this. That this blood appears with its redness is due to the oxygenation process. We can only make a brief reference to this subject here.

If we are now having such a significant point in evolution brought to our attention, through the legend and the Bible as the (*driving forth of Adam and Eve from Paradise and the*) re-entering of Seth into Paradise, then we need to remind ourselves as to how the human being was cast out of Paradise in the first place. The human being was cast out of Paradise, that is to say, out of the old evolutionary state of existing in the lap of the Divine, through the following. The process is indicated in the Bible as a physical process; but this proceeded in parallel with the (*spiritual, ethical*) deterioration (*of the astral body*). Those who wish to understand the Bible have to learn to accept its literal meaning (*in this instance*). It is written: "God breathed the living breath into Man and he became a living soul" (Gen.2:7). This causing of air to be breathed in by human beings, which in this Bible passage is here pictorially described, is a process which was brought about over some millions of years. What does it mean?

There have been phases in human evolution, in the forming of the human body, wherein the body did not as yet possess any lungs; so oxygen could not have been breathed in. In past ages there were phases wherein the human being more or less floated in a fluidic-aquatic environment. In that time, the human being possessed a specific organ, a kind of air-bladder, from which the lungs evolved, in later times. (*This was in the late Hyperborean Epoch on into the early Lemurian Epoch.*) The air-bladder metamorphosed itself into lungs, and one can (*with initiatory clairvoyance*) follow the evolutionary process involved in this. If we do that, then one perceives that this process is that same process which in the Bible is represented pictorially as, "And God breathed the living breath into Adam, and Adam became a living soul". It is with the bringing about of breathing, that the creating of red blood first became possible. In this way, the descent of humanity into a material, flesh body, is connected with the red-coloured 'tree of blood' being produced within the human being.

Picture to yourself, that a person is in front of you and, looking at them, you could only see and follow with your gaze, the droplets of red blood emerging (*from the bone marrow*) and then pulsing along: you would have before you, a living 'red tree'.

This 'tree' is referred to by the Christian esotericist as the "Tree of Knowledge". The human being has 'torn into'[41] the tree; the human being has enjoyed partaking of this red-coloured 'tree of blood'.

> Note: In Biblical language, the human being has enjoyed the inherently destructive process of 'eating' from the fruit of the Tree of Knowledge of Good and Evil. That is, by the astral body becoming aware of, and then being subject to, the earthly sense of self, with its lower drives and urges.

The setting up of the red coloured 'tree of blood', the tree which is the true Tree of Knowledge - this is the primal sin (*called Original Sin in theological terms*), which led directly to the 'Fall of Man', and then the expulsion (*of Adam and Eve*) from the Garden of Eden: "And God drove the man and his help-mate from the Garden, so that the man may not also enjoy partaking of the Tree of Life." (Gen. 3:22-24)

In fact, we have another tree in us, which you can picture to yourselves in a similar way to that of the other tree. But this second tree has bluish-red blood. This blood is the 'substance' of death. This bluish-red tree was implanted in the human being at the same time as the other tree. When the human being lay in the bosom of the Godhead, the Godhead was able from within the human being to intertwine together that which was, in effect his life, with his cognizing capability. In the future, there shall be a time when the human being, through his or her extended consciousness, shall be capable of transforming the blue blood into red blood. When that is possible, then within the human being itself, the fountain (*of astral and etheric renewing energies*) shall exist which can transform the blue blood into a Tree of Life. In our times, it is a Tree of Death. Thus in this seal there lives a view into the past, and on into a view of the future!

You see that in the human being, a red, and a bluish-red, 'blood-tree' are intertwined. The red blood is the expression of the 'I'; the blue blood is the expression of death. The

---

[41] This unusual expression (der Mensch hat gerissen…) implies a tearing at, a clawing at, this wholesome unfallen state of the soul and the life-forces, by the lower human impulses..

blue 'blood-tree' was brought into being in addition to the red 'blood-tree' as punishment (*from God*). In the far future, this Tree of Death shall become transformed into the Tree of Life (*see Commentary below.*) When you think of the human being as you see him or her, the person's entire life in the present is based on the interaction between these two trees.

Notes on the above lecture extract about the two columns

In the far future, this Tree of Death shall become transformed into the Tree of Life.
The lecture notes for the above sentence continues on, with these words: "just as it was originally a Tree of Life".

That the current 'bluish-red 'Tree of Death' was originally a Tree of Life, is a confusing and incorrect statement. For Rudolf Steiner is apparently telling his audience in effect, that the bluish-red 'Tree of Death' once existed as an 'unfallen tree'. Yet it is clear from the lecture that it came into existence already as a debased 'tree' at the same time as the red-blood tree. That is, as people began to breathe, and to perceive their environs, the blood stream became laden with carbon dioxide, forming bluish-red blood. In fact, it was in this lecture that Rudolf Steiner informed his audience, "the bluish-red tree was established in the human being at the same time as the red-blood tree". Consequently, it is clear that the lecture notes which record here that the current bluish-red Tree of Death was "originally a Tree of life" are defective.

"....the droplets of red blood emerging..."
This sentence is ambiguous in German, and could also be translated as:

> Picture to yourself, that a person is in front of you, and looking at them, you could only see and follow with your gaze, their red blood as it ripples along: you would have before you, a living 'red tree'.

But the translation I have given earlier is strongly supported by the sentence just before this one, which emphasizes, as a crucial event, "...the red-coloured 'tree of blood' **being produced within** the human being". And it is also strongly supported by the sentence following it, referring to **"the setting up** of the red coloured tree..." The German text is: Denken Sie sich, der Mensch stünde vor Ihnen und Sie könnten nur das Rieseln des roten Blutes verfolgen... The key verb here, 'rieseln', here can mean 'falling in drops'.

COMMENTARY: SEAL FOUR

The two columns Jachin and Boaz:
These are referred to in all three sources, and are a very prominent feature of the seal, so they will be discussed now.

Boaz: It is known that the word "Boaz" has the meaning of 'strength'.
Jachin: There is no full academic consensus as to the meaning of this word, but generally it is accepted that the name "Jachin" derives from a Hebrew verb for 'setting up' (as in establishing, or consolidating, something).

Rudolf Steiner defines these words in this way:

Boaz: "That which I have sought in myself, the strength - that I shall find throughout the realm in which I will then exist (*when I rise into higher worlds*)". So there is the nuance of "out of the world", and the nuance of **Strength** in this word.[42]

Jachin: "The divine reality which is in thyself and which is poured out into the (*physical*) world".[43] So there is here, the nuance of the inner world, and the nuance of **Wisdom**. Jachin is further explained as referring to "the spiritual energy that imprints Form upon the Formless". Rudolf Steiner also explained Jachin as being "the Creator-Word which invokes the divine-spiritual beings (into activity) within the world." (In German, *Das Schöpfer Wort das die Geistige Wesenheiten in die Welten rufen.*) GA 266b p. 128.

Not permitted to speak these two words
Before we consider these meditative verses, we need to explore Rudolf Steiner's reported words, as published in the German text of the informal lecture given discreetly to a small group on 21st May. Namely that during that lecture, he was not given permission from the spiritual worlds, to actually pronounce these two words (p.53); and secondly, his reported statement that the meaning of these two words is: "I am whom I was, I am who now is, I am who shall be." Firstly, we should note that these two words are in the Bible:

> 1Kings 7:21, "He erected the pillars at the portico of the temple. The pillar to the south he named Jachin and the one to the north Boaz."

So they are pronounced whenever a person reads the Bible aloud, or speaks about this passage with colleagues and friends. There is no general religious tradition against pronouncing these words, unlike the special word designating the name of God. This name was developed from the enigmatic phrase spoken to Moses as the title of God, from the burning bush: "I am whom I was, I am who now is, I am who shall be". This one word, written JHVH, is regarded as too sacred to actually pronounce, but for practical purposes a pronunciation for this word was created.

Also, the names of these columns, Jachin and Boaz, do not literally mean, "I am whom I was, I am who now is, I am who shall be", for this phrase is the accepted translation of three other, entirely different Hebrew words, 'ehyeh asher ehyeh'. These are the words referred to above, which were given by "the Lord God" (i.e., Jahve-Christ) to Moses as His name, when Moses wanted to know the name of this Deity, who was giving him his task of freeing the Hebrews from Egypt. (Exod. 3:14)

---

[42] GA 265 p.352
[43] GA 265 p.352.

So there are two problems with the German text here.

Problem 1

We can now attempt to resolve the point about not being permitted to pronounce these words. In a lecture some years after the Conference, to a small group of Theosophists, who were in a branch (or 'lodge') of the unorthodox Freemason Order led by Rudolf Steiner for some ten years, he reminds them that indeed it is not permitted to pronounce the word, 'Jachin', **when giving a candidate entry to the lodge.**[44] But otherwise, Rudolf Steiner could, and did, pronounce these two words when speaking of a Biblical subject.[45]

That he told his audience in the unofficial, discreet session during the Munich Conference that he was not permitted to speak the words, supports the conclusion mentioned in the Introduction that this session was in fact offered primarily to the Theosophists who were in the unorthodox Freemason Order. Otherwise, there is no taboo against speaking these two words in a normal Theosophical lecture.

Problem 2

We shall now attempt to resolve the point about the words 'Jachin' and 'Boaz' as apparently meaning, "I am whom I was, I am who now is, I am who shall be" and hence being the name of God. This is another place where the lecture notes are corrupted, for it is extremely unlikely that Rudolf Steiner said this, since it is grammatically impossible. Even if he did say this, these words still could not actually have that particular meaning: "*I am whom I was, I am who now is, I am who shall be*". This is indicated by the fact that Rudolf Steiner elsewhere defined 'Jachin' as "a Creator-word", not the name of the Creator.

The solution is found in very brief notes of a private esoteric lesson given to members of this Freemason Order. We learn there that, instead of the legend recounting that a fiery cloud arose from the grave of Adam with the two initials J and B in it, there is another version. In this version, a bush appeared to Seth, in the midst of which were the Hebrew words 'ehyeh asher ehyeh' which God (Jahve) spoke to Moses, and which are normally translated as, "I am who I was, I am who now is, I am who shall be".[46]

So, the above, official, but problematic passage,

> *These are the first letters of two words, the speaking forth of which (here) I am not permitted, by spiritual powers. But the meaning of these words is: "I am whom I was, I am who now is, I am who shall be."*

was very probably something like this:

> These are the first letters of two words, the speaking forth of which I am not permitted, by spiritual powers, if we are in a Freemason lodge meeting.[47] For they are words with a deep spiritual significance.
> Indeed the Temple legend also tells us that from Adam's grave a fiery bush appeared with words in it, words which convey the name of God, as spoken to Moses. These words spoken to Moses, mean, "I am whom I was, I am who now is,

---

[44] GA 265, p 287.

[45] For example, in GA 265, pages 279, 403.

[46] In GA 265, p.342.

[47] It is possible that after various more open themes had been discussed at this 4pm informal session, most of the participants were encouraged to leave, so that the seals could be explained to a smaller group, mostly Freemason Theosophists.

I am who shall be", and the special name of God, which was developed from this sentence, also may never be spoken. This example tells us how significant are the names of these two columns, names which we cannot speak in a formal ceremony.

Identifying the social context of this discreet esoteric session, resolves the inconsistencies, and removes impossible implications, and also permits something else. We recall that the Conference hall did have the two columns erected in it, as if the Conference were to some extent, in a Freemason context, informally. This arrangement inside the hall also affirms that Rudolf Steiner, in speaking the above re-constructed sentence, was emphasizing to the unorthodox Freemasonry members, the sacredness and seriousness of their rituals.

Jachin and Boaz: contemplating the four verses for these

Inscribed around the base of the two columns placed in the hall for the Conference were four brief meditative verses. These could also be considered 'seals', or more accurately 'guideposts'. That is, these four verses exist in the spiritual world, conjured for as important meditative guideposts for the spiritual seeker who is striving to understand the meaning of the two columns, named 'Jachin' and 'Boaz'. We know this, because Rudolf Steiner informed his audience that he made these texts available "in the German language", thereby revealing that he 'read' them in the astral realm in a non-earthly spiritual script. In November of 1907, he gave an 'Esoteric Lesson' on these meditative words to his more advanced students. The brief notes which have survived from this lesson help us to understand the verses,

JACHIN (wisdom) (GA 265 p.403)

In pure thinking you find the self
which can maintain its own being.

When you transform the thought into an image,
you can experience the creative Wisdom.

Jachin is about the more contemplative, meditative pathway that leads to the soul receiving wisdom. As Rudolf Steiner taught, Jachin is about discovering that, "the Divine, which is poured-out over Creation, is within you". (GA 265 p. 352)

1st verse: The expression, 'pure thinking' which can 'maintain its own being', refers to a higher consciousness. So it is pointing towards the development of the Spiritual-self, for this part of our spiritual nature confers an eternal self-hood. The spiritual seeker can achieve eventually an ego-sense which does not fade out when it is exposed to various challenges, and which after death, sustains our cognizing in realms of spirit.

2nd verse: "transform the thought into an image": When we go beyond an intellectual idea (which is often just a mental image) we can attain the state of clairvoyant sensing of the vibrant astral image or living thought-form behind the earthly thought.

BOAZ (strength) (GA 265 p.403)

When you condense the feeling-sensing to light,
then you make manifest the forming Power.

If you actively apply your Will into matter * (*into the material-physical world)
then you are creating in cosmic existence.

3rd verse: "When you condense the feeling-sensing to light": again the brief notes of Rudolf Steiner's teachings to his advanced students on this line are helpful. This line refers to a person 'feeling-sensing' the influence of etheric or astral forces in nature, behind (or present in) a material phenomenon; the most powerful such influences come from the Sun or the Moon. And the verse also indicates how, through meditation, this brings about an enhancement of one's cognitional ability. There is a progression from this sensitive 'feeling-sensing' to clairvoyantly seeing these influences as radiant astral images. Then, eventually, the acolyte can begin to be a source of such formative energies behind material things; the acolyte can even start to ray forth such noble energies from themselves.

4th verse: "...actively apply your Will into matter". This second last line has a complex construction grammatically in German, and is difficult to grasp. Once the subtle German text is understood, one sees that it is conveying this complex, and subtle thought:

if you materialize your will, so that it becomes a specific reality/entity, active in the physical world...then you are creating in the cosmos.
(in German, "Verdinglichst du den Willen zum Wesen").[48]

The veiled message of this line is very significant, and actually applies to the highest level of consciousness: to "High-initiation consciousness" or "Intuition". If the sincere spiritual seeker applies real strength and determination (the 'Boaz' qualities) to the purification and sanctification of their will - the most hidden and most potent aspect of the human soul - then eventually such a person may apply their will to Creation. In doing this, such a person is helping to shape the future world. This advanced state of spirituality requires access to intuitive wisdom existing amongst the gods in upper Devachan. But such a capacity can already start to manifest, to a weaker degree, before such a high clairvoyance is attained.

In Summary

Boaz is the contrasting pathway to that of the more passive and contemplative Jachin path; Boaz concerns direct interaction with the material world and thereby gradually gaining wisdom and skills. It implies that eventually, the ability is attained to be almost a co-creator in the world, with the gods. Boaz and Jachin can also be viewed as alluding to the two great archetypal Biblical sons of Adam: Cain and Abel. Boaz is alluding to Cain and his kindred souls, who have to work their way into spirituality from an earthly, fallen soul, and seek a practical wisdom. Whereas Jachin is alluding to Abel and his kindred souls, who are more contemplative, and who are naturally receptive to high spiritual wisdom.

Water and Earth

Finally there is the evolutionary message of the seal. Rudolf Steiner explained that if the upper part of the seal is depicting humanity in the future, existing beyond the material world, in a radiant, ethereal state, then the two columns refer to earlier evolutionary stages. The red column resting on the water, alludes to the Hyperborean and early Lemurian epochs, when the Earth was fluidic; then humanity existed in an

---

[48] A clearer rendering than, "If you concretize Will to beings, you will create in world existence". (Ref. *6.*)

aquatic environment, and developed a sentient capacity, which manifested as a primitive emotional capacity. But these crude, restless passions and desires can be transformed into a finely sensitive compassion and a discerning awareness of the world around one. This provides the basis for higher spiritual consciousness; especially for 'Inspiration' or 'Cosmic-spiritual consciousness'. These epochs belong to the first half of the Earth Aeon, which is known as the 'Mars' half of the Aeon.

The bluish-red column is placed on solid matter, on the ground; and this alludes to the mid-Lemurian epoch and Atlantean epochs, and also our current epoch, where humanity exists in a solidified, material world. As the human body became more dense, and gradually formed a skeletal system and a covering of protoplasm, the brain could form, and on this basis, the intellect could begin to manifest. But it is the earth-bound, brain-associated ideas or mental pictures, which eat away at the vitality of the soul and the ether body; becoming the 'tree of death'. However, this achievement of developing concepts does provide the basis for a future form of higher spiritual consciousness. This half of the Earth Aeon is known as the Mercury half.

Around the lower periphery of the seal is the Hexagram, which is the symbol of the Life-spirit. The Life-spirit is the outcome of developing the capacity to perceive and then to directly influence what is active behind sense phenomena. This leads to an enhanced artistic capacity and to healing abilities. There is also the Pentagram, the symbol of the Spiritual-self, which is the outcome of developing the capacity for spiritual consciousness or 'pure thinking'. Below, on the seal's border is the symbol of the Sun, whose spiritual forces are seeking to guide the human soul up to these goals. It is also pointing to the remote, distant goal of humanity mentioned in the lecture, "and the human being shall (*in the future*) unite with the Sun and receive higher forces from it."

The human being as a sun being

We are told that the sun image with a face faintly in it, points to the radically transformed state of the human being, in a far future epoch. In that Age, humanity shall exist in a spiritual state, and no longer in a flesh body. It is relevant in this context, to consider that in a passage in the Gospel of St. Matthew, Christ - the high sun-god - is discreetly referring to this same future condition. When the Gospels were written, this future dynamic was a secret known only to initiates, hence such truths were presented in a veiled way;

> "Then the righteous will shine like the sun in the kingdom of their Father. He who has ears, let him hear." Matt. 13: 43.

In particular, it is the inclusion of that special phrase, "He who has ears, let him hear" which tells the alert reader that a privileged, esoteric truth is being partially revealed.

This passage in the New Testament can be viewed as simply a poetic phrase, but it does appear to refer to what this seal is implying. In fact this same idea is found in the deeply esoteric Book of Enoch, where the seer states that in a future Age, the spiritualized human beings, "shall be before Him, as radiant as fiery lights...shining as the lights (*stars*) of heaven". (39:7 & 104:2). The same future state is also referred to in the Book of Daniel, "Those who have wisdom (*the Spiritual-self*) shall shine like the brightness of the heavens." (12:2)

As Rudolf Steiner has made clear, this is referring to a far distant time, but even so it can remain a remote idea, because this teaching, this implication of the seal, is very foreign to our earthly mind-set. In Appendix 2 are two meditations (dates unknown) which provide a helpful pathway to understanding more livingly this esoteric concept of humanity existing within what we could call 'the spiritual sun'. The two meditations introduce us to the idea of a spiritual-sun realm in a more understandable way: as a divine, celestial place where the cosmic sun-god Christ is to be experienced, and as the 'spiritual centre' from where our soul is guided towards the Spiritual-self. This is a help towards grasping the idea of existing on a devachanic solar level in the far future.

SEAL FIVE

Attaining the Spiritual-self

What do we see ?

This seal presents a close replica of a scene described in Revelation. A feminine human being has the Sun radiantly glowing in the waist area, and under her feet is the Moon.

Near her, in a somewhat threatening gesture is a seven-headed, ten-horned serpent.

In her body language, she is guarding herself from the serpent.

Around her head are stars, alluding to the 12 zodiac energies.

This seal is about the higher spiritual qualities slumbering in the human being which shall enable the Lower-self to be substantially, if not fully, overcome, in a future time. One could say, it is about manifesting the Spiritual-sun in oneself, and thereby conquering the lower Powers.

Rudolf Steiner's explanation of Seal 5

A: Written report of the 1907 Munich Congress (GA 34 p. 599)
The fifth seal presents the further development of humanity in the cosmos, in which the conditions that have been indicated shall occur. The human being of the future, who will have a different relationship to the Sun to that which prevails in our times, is represented through, "the woman who was clothed with the Sun" (Rev.12:1). The mastery which the human being of the future shall then have over certain forces of the world, which today manifest in the human being's lower nature, is represented by the woman placed victoriously over the Beast which has seven heads and ten horns. At that future time, the woman will have the Moon under her feet: this is referring to a later cosmic relationship existing between the Sun, Earth and Moon.

B: Conference lecture: 21st May 1907

Note: An error exists in the notes of this lecture, in the German text, and this was placed in the official German book, and then carried through into the English version. The explanations by Rudolf Steiner for Seal 5 have been incorrectly allocated to Seal 6, and the explanations for Seal 6 were allocated to Seal 5.[49] We can confirm these errors by observing for example, that the lecture extract below mentions a feminine entity and the Moon, and a 'solar woman'. All of these features belong to the fifth seal; they are not present at all in seal 6, despite being allocated to seal 6 in the official book.

The Fifth Seal
(Published as referring to seal 6.)
{*With this seal*}, we are gazing at a far future time, where future cosmic conditions are presented, when the human being shall again have achieved further refinement in regard to its external form.[50] We see that the Earth and the Sun have become united, which is in effect the result of the 'Moon-body' having been cast out. You will remember that Goethe called the highest element which the soul can strive towards, "the Eternal-Feminine". That element in human nature which overcomes the no-longer-needed (*lower*) qualities, is described as 'feminine' (*by esoteric wisdom*). When the (*non-material, spiritualized*) Earth has been united to the Sun, then shall the human being become the 'solar woman' (*as depicted here*).

At that point, the human being will have achieved union with the Sun. The un-needed substance (*the lower-self astrality*) is portrayed as the Moon, which has to be trampled underfoot. That which has to be cast out when the Earth is again *(in a state of being compatible with that of th*e) Sun, is portrayed by the (*7-headed*) dragon. (*The Earth shall then be in a condition compatible with the Devachanic level of the solar sphere.*) This Dragon force will have been conquered when the Earth has again become Sun.

C: Lecture, 16th September 1907

The Fifth Seal
{*This seal portrays*} the time which approaches (*after the Age of the fourth seal*), wherein great changes occur in the cosmos. When the human being has drawn unto itself the (*spiritual*) solar qualities (*of the sun gods or Powers as St. Paul calls them*),

---

[49] This confusion is carried over into the official English version, "*Rosicrucianism Renewed*" (Ref.6).
[50] "achieved further refinement": the German text has the literal meaning: 'ascended'.

then the (*spiritualized, non-physical*) Earth will again be united with the Sun. The human being shall become a solar being. The human being shall bring forth a sun (*within their own soul-spiritual body*), through the power of the (*spiritual*) sun. Therefore, in this seal, the human being is depicted as begetting a 'sun'. (*This does not mean an actual astronomical star or sun, but refers to the Life-spirit.*) In that future Age the human being will be so morally and ethically developed, that all pernicious, depraved powers, which are slumbering (*i.e., half-hidden, lying in wait*) in the lower nature of the human being, are conquered.

This lower nature is portrayed by the dragon with seven heads and ten horns. At the feet of the 'solar-woman' is the Moon, which contains all the evil substances which the Earth could not use, and which the Earth (*consequently*) cast out of itself.[51] Everything, in the way of magical powers which the Moon exerts on the Earth shall then be overcome. When the human being is united with the (*spiritual*) Sun, the soul will have overcome the (*negative influences of*) the Moon.

D: From the brief comments in the October 1907 Folio

...certain forces of a lower kind, which exist **within** the human being and which hinder the person from the full unfolding of spirituality, shall by now have been removed from the human being. In the seal, these lower forces are portrayed on the one hand by the beast with "seven heads and ten horns"; and on the other hand, by the Moon at the feet of the solar human being. From the viewpoint of Spiritual Science, the Moon is the central point of certain lower forces which today are still exerting an influence in the human being, and which the human being of the future shall compel to be 'underneath' them. (The word in bold font was emphasized by Rudolf Steiner.)

[51] The commentary refers to an error in the German sentence here, which has been corrected.

COMMENTARY: SEAL FIVE

Solar Woman:

The main figure, a feminine being with the sun in the middle and the moon below, is identified by Rudolf Steiner in these lectures on the seal as the future human being, (not as a goddess, Sophia). So this seal depicts the future human being, in a state wherein the Spiritual-self has been developed, together with some of the immensely radiant Life-spirit. In his commentary, Rudolf Steiner points out that this image alludes to the similar image in Revelation, of the woman with the moon under feet, the sun in her middle area, and the stars above. The Book of Revelation (chapter 12) informs us that she has "twelve stars above her head", this is because they allude to the zodiac constellations, which are so closely linked to our way of thinking, hence to our attitudes and earthly personality. So although three of the stars are hidden behind her head, there are actually 12 stars around her head, representing the zodiac.[52] This feature is telling us that the intelligence of the human being in that future epoch shall be free of earth-bound, ahrimanic qualities; it shall reflect the cosmic intelligence of the hierarchies. Rudolf Steiner taught that in remote Ages, the Hierarchies directed these 12 zodiac streams into the human head so that the human being could be able to think, to manifest intelligence.[53]

The Spiritual-self and the Sophia

In 17 times in some 360 volumes, where Rudolf Steiner refers to 'Sophia', he defines the word Sophia (or Isis), **as meaning the Spiritual-self,** not a goddess:

> The spiritual-soul, in whom the Spiritual-self is developing, is called 'Sophia'.[54]

He explains the reason that the Greeks chose a feminine term 'Sophia' is that,

> The earlier initiates noticed how cosmic energies streamed into the pure newly formed Spiritual-self...and hence they gave a feminine name to this fifth part of the human being ....[55]

In other words, with the clairvoyance bestowed by the Spiritual-self state, the 'Sophia' acolyte felt his or her soul receiving the in-raying energies of the cosmos, and this kind of receiving is a feminine dynamic. There are only two apparent exceptions where Rudolf Steiner refers to Sophia as a goddess. One is in his famous lectures, *The Search for the Isis-Sophia*, which refer to the ancient Egyptian perspective; the name Isis is the equivalent of Sophia. Here Rudolf Steiner explains that in Egypt, on this level, Isis represented the spiritually alive cosmos, as experienced by clairvoyant vision; creation is then imbued with many divine beings, lesser spirits and astral-etheric forces general,

> Isis is the **personified** All-wisdom of *our* world...in her true figure, Isis is permeating the entire cosmos...she is that which shines radiantly towards us in many auric colours from the cosmos...[56]

So from this, it is clear that the 'goddess' Isis is a poetic figure of speech, called a 'personification'. The second occasion was on 6th Feb 1913, when speaking about an

---

[52] There are 12 stars here, pointing to the zodiac, not just nine (the number of the hierarchies). This is also shown by the fact that in the small copy of this seal privately made for a friend, Ms. Rettich painted in 10 stars, leaving just two stars behind the head.

[53] GA 101, lect.of 28th Oct, 1907.

[54] For example, in GA 100, lect. 22. Nov, 1907, GA 94 lect. 25. May 1906 / GA 97, lect. 3rd Feb. 1906 & 2nd Dec. 1906.

[55] Lect. 28th Mar. 1907, in GA 55 p.230.

[56] Lect. 24th Dec. 1910, in GA 202 p.238.

initiation process in ancient Egypt. He describes Isis on another level, as the being who was encountered in a remote, high spiritual realm, from whom core spiritual aspects of the human being derive. But before speaking about this aspect of Isis, he first refers to this 'deity' as 'real substantialities' and thereafter as a 'being'. So, also here, the view of Isis as an identifiable, separate entity is not emphasized. This is because in reality there are three distinct types of this Isis. These three are presented in Egyptian art, and include a severe, lion-faced deity. However, we need to note that in later Egyptian times and especially by the Hellenistic Age, popular religious folklore presented Isis as a specific goddess, with various earthly functions and achievements, such as creating fruit-bearing plants to nurture human beings.

With regard to the less remote, spirit-permeated, enchanting 'Isis-Sophia cosmos', this is depicted by Rudolf Steiner in his new image for the zodiacal sign of Virgo, which he designed as part of a new series of zodiacal images. These zodiac images were painted onto the ceiling of the Anthroposophical Centre in Stuttgart in 1912.[57] So generally Rudolf Steiner teaches that creation, as experienced by a person developing higher consciousness, takes on a radiant, en-souled quality, and this quality is poetically thought of as specific entity, a goddess. It is precisely this wonderful vista which is called Isis or Sophia. In addition, as we noted above, the Spiritual-self level of consciousness - which allows one to perceive this vista - is also called Isis or Sophia. We need to be clear that the word 'personification' means that a quality or an experience, is especially presented as if this were a living being. This literary device was used very extensively in earlier esoteric texts and in Christian religious texts, until recent times.

Personification

In literary usage, personification is a device wherein human traits and qualities, such as emotions, intelligence, or intentions, are given to physical objects or to natural phenomena, etc. William Shakespeare personified many things; for example, the early dawn: "the morn, in russet-coloured mantle clad, walks o'er the dew of yon eastward hill". Some other examples can be: 'the dark clouds scowled at us', or 'the westerly wind whispered stories of the sea to the old fisherman'.

But in addition to this, initiatory texts can 'personify' something in a more esoteric way. The initiates of earlier Ages could personify the wisdom present in the Spiritual-self, as well as various soul moods or feelings, such as repentance or yearning. They could also personify a way of thinking, or an intention in someone's will. They used this literary device because the astral dynamics in the soul appear in the spiritual worlds as a corresponding astral 'thought-form' or 'feeling-form'. These astral forms are not deities, however they are distinct forms. This personifying of higher wisdom, as a potential within the soul, is seen in the Hellenistic Gnostic texts of the Nag Hammadi library. Such Gnostic accounts of a 'Sophia' are described by Rudolf Steiner as "allegorical-mystical stories"; that is, in these esoteric texts too, Sophia is a personification of divine wisdom, and not a goddess.[58]

When initiates had this experience of a living cosmos, and become deeply permeated by this living, radiant spiritual world all around them, they were often identified by people in their community as an integral part of that same facet of the Divine; so they were also a 'Sophia'. In earlier ages, this was a wide-spread cultural practice amongst mystical-esoteric communities. So, again we see that in esoteric texts, 'Sophia' refers

[57] This building was destroyed in 1937, but this zodiac can been seen, re-constructed from old photographs, in my book, *The Lost Zodiac of Rudolf Steiner.*

[58] This is made clear in a lecture from 29th March 1902, and also from 28th Dec. 1913.

either to the Spiritual-soul, or to the enchanting, spirit-permeated cosmos that such a soul sees.

A religious text from about the time of Christ (*Joseph and Aseneth*) echoes this esoteric awareness in a faint way, when it personifies the quality or mood of repentance, "For Repentance, is an exceedingly beautiful and good daughter, in the heavens". The 'Wisdom' literature of the Bible (such as the *Book of Proverbs*) has large sections devoted to reverence and gratitude for the wisdom which exists in the soul, or which permeates creation. To express the deep feelings that the experience of this wisdom stirs in the soul, the writer of Proverbs would personify the wisdom, which is poetically presented as a 'person', (wisdom is called Chokmah in Hebrew, and later called Sophia, in Greek). Both here and in all similar Biblical texts, Sophia is a **personification** of either the living quality of wisdom in the advanced soul, or the living wisdom permeating creation, as perceived by the advanced soul. Such wisdom is a heritage of the wisdom which during the Moon Aeon had permeated creation.[59] The writer of *Proverbs* reveals understanding of this fact, declaring that Jehovah created this wisdom, that is, God invoked wisdom into the world, "The Lord JHVH brought me forth as the first of His works" (Prov. 8:22).

With regard to this seal, in various lectures Rudolf Steiner referred to our current 5th Post-Atlantean Age as a preparation for the next Post-Atlantean Age, the 6th Age, starting in AD 3573. In the future 6th Age, some of humanity will have the 'Sophia' quality more developed and therefore they will experience all around them, an enlivened cosmos. In a lecture from 1904, when commenting on the 6th Post-Atlantean Age he again defines 'Sophia' as the wisdom state of the Spiritual-self and not a goddess. His remarks were noted briefly as:

> "The 6th cultural Age, which we now are preparing for. Within the Age of Sophia or Wisdom, (*we shall be preparing for the 7th cultural Age)*; for direct knowledge of God: that is, Theosophy.
> The 7th cultural Age: (*we shall then manifest*) practical Theosophy: accomplishing the practical application of what we spiritually know.[60]

Mary, mother of Jesus

A theory has developed around Mary, namely that she had a goddess in her aura. But Rudolf Steiner taught that, "Mary, who gave birth to Jesus, had developed the Spiritual-self, and **for this reason she was called "Sophia" by the early Christians**".[61] Likewise, when speaking about the Book of Revelation in 1909, Rudolf Steiner reported that in the ancient Egyptian culture, acolytes or initiates who were at the stage of the Spiritual-self and drawing near to experiencing the Sun god, could be called "Isis" (i.e., Sophia, in Greek) – meaning they had developed the Spiritual-soul:

> "Isis is the name for the soul who is seeking the sun-spirit, Osiris." [62]

So Mary was regarded as a 'Sophia' person because she had acquired the stage of Spiritual-self. That the term 'Sophia' does not refer to a goddess is a situation which Rudolf Steiner emphasized when speaking of this seal. He reminded his audience of a famous phrase from Goethe, which has a feminine figure in it "You will remember that

---

[59] The view of S. Prokofieff (p, 39, *The Heavenly Sophia and the being, Anthroposophia*) that various hierarchical beings in their activity during the Sun Aeon had created a goddess 'Sophia' is a theory for which no evidence is offered. In fact, it contradicts the above-mentioned teachings of R. Steiner on 'Sophia'. Consequently, Prokofieff's theory that "Sophia gave birth to Christ" in the Sun-sphere has no basis.

[60] Lecture, 16.6.1904.

[61] GA 97 p.58.

[62] GA 104A lect., 15th May 1909.

Goethe called the highest element which the human soul can strive towards, "the Eternal-Feminine". It appears from Rudolf Steiner's work, that there are specific divine beings with either feminine, masculine or neutral qualities, but Sophia is a term for the interweaving of a range of divine energies and beings. With regard to our Spiritual-self, he taught that this derives, at least initially, from the highest of the Angels. This Angel was called "The Holy Spirit" in antiquity, (but this title is also used of other beings, with whom this highest Angel may interweave its energies). Whereas the Life-Spirit derives from the highest of the Archangels, who is associated with the sun-god, Christ.[63]

Goethe's the "Eternal-Feminine" (p. 68)

> This reference is to poetic words of Goethe in the 'Chorus Mysticus' from his play, *Faust*, Part Two. At the very end of this great drama, a mystical chorus of 'spirit voices' declare the nature of the Spiritual-self, "The Eternal-Feminine draws us onwards !" (Das Ewig-Weibliche zieht uns hinan !)

...**and which the Earth** (consequently) **cast out of itself** (p. 69)

The official German sentence from the lecture of Sept. 16th states, when translated,

> "the solar woman conquered the Moon...which contains all the evil substances that the Earth could not use, ***and which the Earth had <u>not</u> cast out of itself.***"

This confusing text implies some theoretical, second source of lunar material still in the Earth, which "the Earth had **not** cast out of itself", and which the future human being conquers. But the word 'not' is clearly an error. For such malignant substances and energies were specifically cast out of the Earth in Lemurian times, thereby forming the Moon. So it follows that the last part of the sentence is actually this: "and which the Earth (did) cast out of itself". That there is an error in the German sentence, and that there is no secondary lunar material implied, is clearly confirmed by the words spoken in the lecture of May 21st, "*The un-needed substance (the lower-self qualities) is portrayed as the Moon, which has to be trampled underfoot.*" There is no reference here to a **second source** of malignant lunar influences, and there is no depiction in the seal of a secondary source of lunar material.

7 Heads, 10 Crowns

The deep esoteric meaning behind this extraordinary figure, well-known to readers of Revelation, remained a riddle until Rudolf Steiner gave a series of majestic lectures about this book, in 1908; *The Apocalypse of St. John.* The lectures need to be read, to really immerse one's soul in the message of the seal; but here we can outline the meaning. It was in the Atlantean epoch that the four apocalyptic Group-souls manifested in the physical appearance of human beings. This came to expression in the first four cultural ages of Atlantis; but then in the last three Atlantean cultural ages, three additional types of animal astrality also exerted their influence in the human soul. The feminine figure in the seal depicts the human being who has attained to the Spiritual-self in the Jupiter Aeon; whereas the 7-headed dragon depicts those seven animal influences of the past which have been cast out of the advanced human soul, but which oppress the ascending, or spiritualizing, branch of humanity. The 10 heads allude to the further impact of these seven malignant influences in the human being's physical-etheric body. Finally, we learn from the defensive gesture of the human figure in this seal, that in the future Aeon which it refers to, these evil influences are not fully removed from the cosmos. That shall happen in the following Aeon, known as the Venus Aeon.

---

[63] In Lecture 17th March 1907 (GA 97) and 3rd June 1907 (GA 99).

SEAL SIX

Triumph over the Lower-self

Help from the Archangel Michael

What do we see ?

An Archangelic figure, but with a somewhat human countenance, is holding aloft a key, and also restraining an enchained Dragon.

This image is closely related to a scene in Revelation, wherein the Archangel Michael seizes the Dragon and casts him into an abyss, locking him up in there.

Four symbols are placed around the black border: two pentagrams, a hexagram and the Christian cross.

This seal is presenting a message about the help given to humanity by the Archangel Michael, and how in the far future, evil shall be overcome.

There is also the implication here that human beings, in seeking spirituality, can become attuned to, and even a vessel of, the will of this majestic Archangel.

Rudolf Steiner's explanation of Seal 6

A: Written report of the 1907 Munich Congress (GA 34, p. 599)

The Sixth Seal
The sixth seal presents the human being in a further state of development, with even greater powers (*than those indicated in Seal 5*) over the lower forces of the cosmos. The way that the seal presents this reality bears resemblance to Christian esoteric knowledge: the Archangel Michael holds the enchained dragon.

B: Conference lecture: 21st May 1907

Note: As noted earlier, in the official German and English books, the explanations by Rudolf Steiner for Seal 6 were allocated to Seal 5, and the explanations about Seal 5 were erroneously allocated to Seal 6. We can confirm that this is an error by noting, for example, that the lecture extract below mentions "conquering a dragon", and "evil being enchained". These features belong to this sixth seal; they are not present at all in seal 5, despite being allocated to seal 5 in the official book.

The Sixth Seal
Lecture, 21st May 1907
(Published as referring to seal 5.)
On the sixth seal we have a being who conquers the dragon. This is the future human being who has completely enchained the so-called lower element (*of human nature*). This stage is connected with cosmic conditions, when that which we call 'Kama' has been trodden under the feet.

(*"Kama", not 'karma", which means 'lower desires' in Sanskrit.*)

C: Lecture, 16th September 1907

The Sixth Seal
In the sixth seal is portrayed for us how the human being, who has ascended to a high level of spirituality, is similar to the figure of (*Archangel*) Michael; how he has enchained what is evil in the world, (*presented here in*) the symbol of the enchained dragon.

D: From the brief comments in the October Folio

The Sixth Seal
Seal 6 portrays the purified, and, not only spiritualized, but ***highly*** spiritualized, human being. A person who has not only conquered the lower forces (*in the soul*) but has so transformed them, that they are now available, as greatly improved forces, for his or her use in their tasks. That the beast is ***tamed***, points to this dynamic.

(Emphasis from Rudolf Steiner)

In the Revelation of St. John, one reads,

> "And I beheld how an Angel descended from heaven, who held the key to the Abyss, and also a great chain in his hand. And he seized the dragon, that ancient serpent, who is the devil, or Satan, and bound him for a thousand years."

COMMENTARY: SEAL SIX

We have only these four brief paragraphs about this seal.

A: with powers over the lower forces of the cosmos
So here the human being has progressed beyond seal 5, where the effort had to be made to repel the evil influences in oneself. For now the human being shall have completely conquered the Lower-self, and "the lower forces of the cosmos". This second point is very significant. For as the human being purifies the soul, achieving high spirituality, the human being is also ennobling the planetary spheres. Our soul qualities derive from the planetary spheres, and are always livingly connected to the planets; so our 'inner work' has an 'outer' impact. The microcosm is affecting the macrocosm.

B: Kama will be conquered
These words point to a very important dynamic which the words of Rudolf Steiner in the folio imply: that as the Lower-self or 'Kama' is conquered, it is itself actually being transformed. The emergence of 'Manas' (an alternative term for the Spiritual-self) is brought about by the transformation of the lower astral qualities; kama re-appears, after being ennobled and imbued with the Christ-light, as the Spiritual-self. (This truth is shown in Rosicrucian inspired fairy tales, when the Prince appears in splendour, after a bear skin around him is removed.)

C: like Archangel Michael
Rudolf Steiner comments that the human being depicted on the seal is, "similar to the figure of (*Archangel*) Michael". The essential point here is that the entire Book of Revelation has several different layers of hidden meaning. The symbolism has to be applicable to these three layers; so at times it has to be somewhat 'strained'. The role of the Archangel is applicable to another layer of meaning, the sequence of historical events, when this great Archangel exerts an influence in the cultural-spiritual evolution of humanity, such as in 1879 when a short Michael-ic phase began. But in his lecture, Rudolf Steiner was not including that level of meaning; he restricts his comments to the over-all spiritual evolving of the human soul. When a human being conquers the Dragon, this is an activity which is similar to the task undertaken since remote Ages, by the great Archangel. But also it is deeply true that Michael seeks to directly help the spiritual seeker in her or his inner battle for a higher spirituality.

The geometric figures around the seal

The **pentagram**, as we noted earlier, is the symbol of the Spiritual-self. In this seal it appears twice, on the left and the right. This may be pointing to what Rudolf Steiner referred to as the "not only spiritualized, but ***highly*** spiritualized, human being..." That is, the doubling of this symbol is intended to emphasize this situation, of the human being having fully conquered the 'Kama' astrality and fully achieved the Spiritual-self.

The **hexagram**, positioned at the prominent overhead point of the seal, implies that the Life-spirit is gaining strength now. This is where 'The Son of Man' initiate rises up to 'The Son of God' rank, as we mentioned earlier.

The **cross** at the bottom of the seal is no doubt telling the viewer that the entire process is being sustained by the Christ-impulse providing the foundations of the spiritual renewal of the human being which the initiatory path offers. That is, from the Christ light are derived the new spiritual qualities of the human being, as Rudolf Steiner so often emphasized in his life's work.

SEAL SEVEN

Becoming a servant of the Grail

The Philosopher's Stone

What do we see ?

We need to note firstly, that this seal is about a particularly sacred theme, because it alludes to complex processes involved in a person becoming attuned to the Holy Grail.

There is a darkened part of the blue central area containing a cube, as well as the lower parts of two serpents.

The energies of the serpents are permeating the cube, and yet despite this, the heads of the serpents rise up and become two luminous spirals.

In the upper area of the blue field, various features are depicted. These are, the upper part of the serpents, which are now more pleasant, and also a dove and a rainbow, as well as an inverted chalice.

Around the perimeter, in the black border, are the letters referring to the Rosicrucian maxims:

Ex Deo Nascimur	In Christum Morimur	Per Spiritum Sanctum Revivismus
From God we are born	Into Christ we die	By the Holy Spirit we are resurrected

This seal both unveils and veils many profound secrets of the way to high spirituality. One could sum up the message of this seal by saying that it is about the soul becoming transformed, to become a vessel of the Christ-light, and thereby a microcosmic reflection of the Christ-imbued solar system.

D N J C M P S S R E

Since seal seven is about the Holy Grail, which is a complex and highly esoteric subject, before my Commentary, there will be a short over-view of what the Holy Grail is, and which aspect of it is emphasized in Rudolf Steiner's explanations.

The Holy Grail

The medieval Holy Grail legends, in their fascinating and inspiring narratives, present several different definitions of this especially sacred theme. The Grail can be the actual cup used at the Last Supper, as recorded by St. Matthew (26:27-28),

Then he took the cup, gave thanks and offered it to the disciples, saying, "Drink from it, all of you. This is my blood of the covenant, which is poured out for many, for the forgiveness of sins.

The Grail can also be presented as an emerald stone, fallen from the crown of Lucifer. This view arises from amalgamating the Grail story by Wolfram von Eschenbach, and the references found in the poem about the medieval Minnesingers Wartburg Contest. This description of the Grail is indicating that influences from Lucifer brought about the earthly sense of self, since green is the colour of the earthly world with its mantle of green plants; so in the legend this colour symbolizes the earthly personality. But when a person seeks to achieve spirituality - and to do this, the essential basis is to have an "I", a sense of self - then that person is transforming the influences of Lucifer. In this way, the general green-ness of the earthly reality, the earthly "I", becomes a precious gem: the beautiful emerald. This precious gem is an expression of Virgo forces; and Virgo at its highest level represents chasteness, soul-purity, that is, the Spiritual-self.[64]

The Grail can be portrayed as the physical blood of Jesus (a small amount of this preserved in a cup), invoking redemption and sanctification into the soul.

It can also be a mysterious chalice, and yet also a kind of healing force and soul nourishment.

The various Grail versions present these different views of this theme, for they are texts designed to uplift and inspire the wider community, so they all refrain from actually defining what is meant esoterically, by 'the Holy Grail". The actual esoteric secret of the Grail was only unveiled in the teachings of Rudolf Steiner. Hence in the medieval books, the Holy Grail is a mysterious and enticing topic, imbued with sacredness, but in many respects remaining unclear. The Holy Grail is such a veiled topic because it is the most sacred of all spiritual mysteries; it can be understood and experienced through a slow, graduated approach to spiritual development. Although some aspects of what is deeply sacred have to remain a mystery, until one unveils it for oneself, through a deep meditative engagement with the legends and Rudolf Steiner indications, the meaning of the Grail does become much clearer.

In my book, *The Vidar Flame-Column, its meaning from Rudolf Steiner*, the profound themes that take us to the core of the Grail mystery are presented in some detail. Here we can briefly note that the essence of the Grail mystery is connected to the absorbing into the soul of radiance, or divine spiritual energies. which ray forth from Christ Jesus. There is no higher level of spirituality than becoming, in one's soul and spirit, a vessel of this gift from the Saviour; in this sense, it is the human being who becomes

---

[64] This emerald stone is prominent in the extraordinary painting, designed by Rudolf Steiner and painted by Anna May, presented in my, *Rudolf Steiner's Esoteric Christianity in the Grail painting by Anna May*. For the zodiacal correspondence of gemstones, see my *Rudolf Steiner Handbook*.

the vessel of the grail, the chalice. For then the core of the Grail mystery can be understood as the human being becoming attuned to, or merging with, Christ.[65]

But in his commentary on the seal, Rudolf Steiner focuses on two aspects of the Grail. One is the raising of one's consciousness from an earth-bound existence with merely logical thinking, to a directly spiritual consciousness, to directly cognizing divine realms. The second aspect is spiritualizing and etherealizing the physical body; this involves gaining the ability to manifest life itself, or generating life-renewing powers by overcoming, to some degree, the physiological aspects of the death process.

Rudolf Steiner's explanation of Seal 7

Note: the following teachings are a special gift to humanity. They provide revelations about some of the deepest secrets of the Grail Mysteries. As mentioned earlier, the notes are corrupt in places and also very brief, so I have found it necessary to add some comments inside the text; these are placed inside brackets, or added as **Notes**. Also, in the Commentary following these lecture extracts, other points in the lecture are explored and clarified. You may also encounter sentences or phrases which are rather baffling; I have not marked these places, as there are too many. But in my Commentary, I have attempted to deal with these, to clarify their intended meaning.

A: Written report of the 1907 Munich Congress (GA 34, p. 599)

The seventh seal is that of the Mystery of the Grail; depicted in the way that it resonated with the esoteric stream which began in 14th century (*the Rosicrucian stream*). In the seal there is depicted a cube, representing the spatial world. From out of all sides of this cube, cosmic serpents come forth - these represent the higher (*spiritual*) forces, but which are (*currently*) living out an existence within the lower (*part of creation*). Coming out from the serpents are cosmic pathways, depicted as spirals: these pathways are symbols of purified and cleansed cosmic forces. Originating from these is the "Holy Grail", and facing this is the Dove. All of this is pointing to - and in an entirely appropriate way - the secret of the bringing the Cosmos into being[66] (*within one's own soul and spirit*). The producing of the earthly[67] is a lower reflection of this process. The deepest mysteries are placed in the lines and general features of this seal.

B: Conference lecture: 21st May 1907

The Seventh Seal

{*Referring back to seal Six, when "Kama is conquered"*} the condition which then enters, when this is achieved, is symbolized by the Holy Grail, as depicted in the last seal. The transparent cube below represents a transparent diamond cube, which consists entirely of carbon. When the human being has progressed so far that he or she can themselves make use of the carbon (*in the body*) for the maintenance of their body (*i.e., the creating of new cells*) - without any participation of the plants - then such a person shall produce this cube. This cube, made of crystallized, pure, carbon is the best

---

[65] Further aspects to the Grail are presented in my book, "Rudolf Steiner on Leonardo's *Last Supper*".
[66] "bringing the Cosmos into being": the German text here is literally, *"the cosmos-begetting"*.
[67] 'producing of the earthly': literally: 'of the earthly-begetting'.

indicator as to the nature of this future state of the human being. (*Diamonds are crystals are made of pure carbon, and thus indicate in some ways, the nature of the future rejuvenated body; especially in their transparency.*) Then the human being will be so advanced, that he shall not only cognize the three dimensions, but also the counter-dimensions which exist as counter-parts to these. For this reason the image in the seal includes the other three, as a kind of reflected image of the three (*physical*) dimensions. These counter-dimensions portray what the human being shall achieve in the future, when through the spirit, it has overcome the physical element. The serpents signify the developing upwards (*by a person*) to the higher (*spiritual*) reality.

Indicated in the seal by finely detailed, coloured imagery, this spiritual ascending is depicted as the violet spirals (*of the serpents).* This finely detailed imagery[68] - the serpentine spirals - signify the devotional, self-sacrificing nature of intuitive, spiritual cognizing (*aspiring up towards the spirit*). Only to this devotional soul-nature is it granted to comprehend the cosmic spirals in the Staff of Mercury, which then (*upon being inwardly grasped in their deeper significance*) become fiery, and which then wend their way spirally upwards, impelled by **a purely spiritual cognizing**.

> **Note**: The higher, more spiralling pathways are painted in a pale, but fiery, pink. There is no full Staff of Mercury here, but the upper spirals do suggest this staff. Also, see the Commentary about these last words, "a purely spiritual cognizing".

Gradually these ascending lines of spiritual energies transform into the Chalice, but one which is turned downwards. The plant chalice is today chaste, and directed upwards, in an unconstrained manner. The pure human being, the human being who has become chaste and innocent, is represented here by the dove. The rainbow signifies the human being who has integrated the sevenfold planetary creative powers.

C: Lecture, 16th September 1907

The Seventh Seal

To the esotericist who knows our world, space is something quite different to what it is for the physical world, namely an emptiness: for space is the fountain, out of which all beings have crystallized, so to speak. Think of a glass cube, which you can see right through, filled with water. Then visualize to yourself that certain currents, which are able to cool the water down, are led through the water in such a way that ice forms. In this way you can experience a mental picture of the creating of the (*physical*) world. The divine Creative Word is spoken into the 'space' - and all things and beings are thereby crystallized (*out of space, into matter; that is, out the ethers, into the spatial, physical world.*)

The esotericist portrays this space, into which the divine Creative Word is spoken, by a cube, as clear as water.[69] This cube is best described like this: it has three vertical directions or axes: length, height and width - so the cube represents the three dimensions of space. And now just consider that there can be included with these three dimensions there in external space, three counter-dimensions.

---

[68] Omitted in the English translation, Rudolf Steiner describes these spirals as "Lichtbild"; he is probably using this word in its rare usage, referring to 'Daguerreotype' photography, (famous for obtaining remarkably detailed images) and meaning thereby the very fine graphic details in the seal. However, it may be that he is using it in a unique, literal usage, which would simply mean 'radiant graphics'.

[69] The text is corrupted here. It is "*In this space, various beings develop. Those beings who are nearest to us we can best characterize as: the cube has three vertical directions or axes.....*" These words have no clear meaning: as they are fragments from one or more incomplete sentences.

(*In regard to the human being*) you can visualize these (*twice three dimensions in the following way*): a human being goes along in a particular direction, and another human being comes towards him, and the two collide. In a similar way, there exists for every spatial dimension, a counter dimension: therefore, (*in this mental image of two people*) we have six rays (*or lines of force*). The other counter-rays together portray the primal seed-bud of the highest members of the human being (*that is, the Spiritual-self, the Life-spirit and the Spirit-human*). The physical body, crystallized out of space, is the lowest member. The highest (*member*), the spiritual element, is the counterpart to this: this spiritual element is depicted (*in the seal*) by these counter-dimensions. Here (*in this seal*) are forming in an initial sense, these counter-dimensions of a human being. They are being depicted here in their developmental process, which one can best portray by allowing them to flow together to form a world of lower passions, lusts and baser instincts (*depicted as serpents*).

> **Note**: The above sentence is somewhat unclear and incomplete. It can be re-constructed in this way: Here in this seal are depicted the counter dimensions as debased qualities, (*in the lower part of the serpents*); these are the lower, un-refined qualities of the human being. This portrays the lowly stage they have so far reached, within the course of humanity's evolution. They represent the veiled counter-dimensions of human nature (e.g., *the threefold Double*) at an initial, rudimentary stage. But in this seal, in the middle-upper section of the seal, these qualities are also portrayed in their future, purified, transformed state – higher spiritual qualities – as radiant 'serpents-becoming-spirals'.

So this is what these serpents are. Lowly at first, but at a later time they are transformed into something else (*higher*). These lower energies become ever more and more purified - we have already seen (*in the earlier seals*) to what heights (*the human being can arise to, when purified*). But these higher qualities originally proceed from lower drives, which are here symbolized by the serpents. This over-all process (*of a gradual transformation*) is symbolized by the merging of the counter-dimensions into two serpents, placed opposite each other.

> **Note**: It is helpful here to know that Rudolf Steiner taught that the snake has been used as the symbol of the self which does not remain just within itself, its own earthly ways of being, but rather can selflessly take up into itself the divine; can sacrifice itself, by transforming itself.

As the human being purifies itself, it rises up to what one calls the 'cosmic spirals'. These cosmic spirals, depicted as the purified body of the serpents, have a deep significance. You can get an idea of this significance from the following situation.... (*fragmentary, corrupted comments about Copernicus are omitted, see Commentary*)... the Sun **also** moves (*not just the Earth and the Moon*).[70] The Sun is indeed in movement, and in fact, it moves in a spiral motion; and thus the Earth, with the Sun, moves in a complicated, curved trajectory. The same complex motion also involves the Moon, which moves around the Earth. These movements are much more complex than one assumes in basic astronomy.

You can, (*if you meditate upon this seal*) perceive how the spirals have their significance with regard to the celestial bodies (*in our solar system*): for these celestial bodies represent a (*living, mobile*) form, a form with which the human being shall identify in

---

[70] The text continues, "astronomy has left out a third postulate of his because it is not considered relevant." This third postulate concerns astronomical theories of no relevance to the theme of the lecture.

the future (*i.e., shall have an inner resonance with; see Commentary*). In that future Age, the human being's reproductive power shall have become purified, cleansed; and then the larynx shall be the reproductive organ. That which the human being shall have developed as a purified 'serpent-body' shall no longer be exerting an influence from below upwards, but rather from above, downwards. The transformed larynx in us shall become the chalice, which one calls 'the Holy Grail'. And likewise just as the one element will be cleansed, so too the other element will be cleansed (*the cosmic matrix of our astral body: the planetary energies*); this element is connected to the 'begetting' organ. Thus shall the reproductive power (*of the human being*) become an extract of the Cosmic Power, of the great (*creative*) Cosmic Essence.

This cosmic Spirit, in its essence, is portrayed by the image of the Dove, which is facing the Holy Grail. Here the dove is the symbol of spiritualized fertilizing, which is effected from out of the cosmos, once the human being has identified itself with the cosmos. The over-all creative element of this process is portrayed by the Rainbow. This is the all-encompassing seal of the Holy Grail.

This seal in its entirety, depicts the purpose behind the inner connection between the human being and the cosmos: in doing this, the seventh seal in effect summarizes the messages of the other seals. For this reason, the Cosmic Secret is presented here as an inscription on the outer edge of the seal. This Cosmic Secret presents how the human being in the beginning was born from out of the primal Powers of the cosmos. Every human being, when it gazes back into its remote past, sees how he or she went through that process in the beginning of time. The human being of today also goes through this process, when he or she is born anew out of their own (*higher*) powers of consciousness (*and becomes an initiate*). This is signified in Rosicrucianism by the letters:

EDN: Ex Deo Nascimur: From God we are born.

> **Note**: There now follows, in this lecture, some meditative words of deep initiatory wisdom on a sacred theme of the Rosicrucian-anthroposophical movement. The Mystery of Golgotha as an event which inaugurated a process that brings release to human beings from the power of death. This means, release from the influence of debased spiritual powers which prevent the individual human being attaining to an eternal spiritual consciousness.

We have seen how within the revelation (*that is, the messages of the seals*) a second element is added: to Life, Death is added, in order that the human being, in this death, can find life again. (*That is, the reality of earthly mortality impels the spiritually awakened person to actively seek an eternal "I".*)[71] The human being must overcome this sensory death in the Primal Fountain of All that is Living. And in fact this Primal Fountain {*the Mystery of Golgotha*} is the central point of all cosmic evolution. For {*underlying the entire drama of the purpose of humanity's existence is the fact that*} we had to experience death, in order to attain to our {*true, eternal*} consciousness. And we shall overcome death then, when we discover the actual reason for, or the purpose of, this {*fact of death being part of human existence*} **in the secret of the Redeemer.**

> **Note**: there now follows the German text of this initiation wisdom, for those who would like to refer to the original text.

---

[71] Which is why in the1616 Rosicrucian illustration, the 'Mons Philosophorum', a grave is shown at the base of the mountain.

Der Mensch muß, damit er in diesem Tod das Leben wiederfindet, in dem Urquell alles Lebendigen diesen Sinnestod überwinden. Und dieser Urquell ist der Mittlepunkt aller kosmischen Entwickelung, denn wir mußten den Tod finden, um unser Bewußtsein zu erringen. Aber wir werden ihn überwinden dann, wenn wir den Sinn dieses Todes im Erlöser-Geheimnis finden.

Just as we are born from God (EDN): so also, we die into Christ, in the sense of esoteric wisdom:

ICM In Christum Morimur: Into Christ we die[72]

And because there, where a duality manifests, a third element must unite with this, so then, the human being, when he or she has overcome death, will be able to identify themselves with the Spirit which permeates creation {*symbolized by the dove*}." The person shall be resurrected and live again, in the spirit: PSSR

"Per Spiritum Sanctum Reviviscimus, 'By the Holy Spirit we are resurrected'."

> **Note**: In the comments made in the lecture of 21st May, the dove is said to represent the human being who is spiritually developed, whereas here the dove represents the Holy Spirit. The apparent contradiction is resolved when one views the spiritualized human being as having attained their sanctification through the influences of the Holy Spirit.

D: The Portfolio from October 1907

...that which forms itself, in respect of the human being, from out of the spatial world, undergoes an evolution from the lower to the higher. From out of the 'three dimensions' - which is portrayed by the cube - there develops at first the lower human qualities. These lower forces are depicted by the serpents, from out of which the now higher, purified, nature is produced; this higher quality is depicted in the cosmic spirals. Through these higher qualities growing and developing into higher levels, the human being can become a vessel suitable for receiving the chaste, spiritual, cosmic being-ness, depicted by the dove. Through this process, the human being becomes a person who has gained mastery over spiritual cosmic powers; these powers are represented by the rainbow. This is a brief outline of this seal, in which there are infinite depths of meaning; these depths can be manifested to those who allow the message of this seal to exert an influence upon the soul, by meditating upon the seal in a devotional manner....In the Rosicrucian maxims, indicated by the letters inscribed upon the periphery of the seal, the full meaning of human development is indicated.

From the lecture of 19th May: about the Cube or Philosopher's Stone

> **Note**: this lecture, given earlier in the Conference, focussed on the seven stages of spiritual development that was inaugurated in medieval times by the first Rosicrucians. In this pathway, the spiritual exercise for developing the 'Philosopher's Stone' or a purified, etherealized physical body, was the fourth stage of seven stages. Rudolf Steiner's comments are invaluable for further understanding of this enigmatic theme.

---

[72] The actual Latin is, In Christo Morimur, but Rudolf Steiner has pointed out that the dative case "In Christum Morimur", (into Christ we die) expresses the meaning of the phrase better than the traditional Latin form which means, 'in Christ we die'; for this can obscure its actual meaning.

(Rudolf Steiner's lecture extract about the Philosopher's Stone)

Modern scholarship has turned this idea (*of the Philosopher's Stone of the medieval alchemists*) into a tale of empty fantasy. But these scholars actually are justified in this, from one point of view. For if the 'Philosopher's Stone' really were what **they** understand it to be, then it would indeed be only a childish idea. But in fact, it is the highest thing that a human being can aspire to achieve. Towards the end of the 18th century, some of the knowledge of the Rosicrucians was betrayed. In this betrayed material we find something, about which we can say, the people of that time certainly encountered some potent ideas !

In fact we find a remarkable report about this in a German newspaper. In this report we are told that; "the Philosopher's Stone exists, and if one can be aware of the full power of this stone, then one has possession of the secret of immortality. And actually most people know this stone; many have it in their hands, daily." The person who wrote this had not the slightest idea as to what it is all about; but he had received information which contained some accurate statements. To resolve this enigma we need only consider the process which maintains, cosmically, human beings of this present time; the process of breathing.

We breathe in and out. We breathe in the oxygen in the air, and we exhale back to the environs the carbon dioxide; a poisonous gas in which we could not live. A plant continuously absorbs this gas, but retains the carbon in the carbon dioxide, from which it builds its own body. However the plant gives out the oxygen to animals and humans. In this way, the plants, animals and humans form a unity, from the viewpoint of the breathing process. In today's world the human being needs the plants. The corpse of the plants is the black coal, which we dig out of the ground, or which we extract as clear diamonds from the ground. This is a substance which we have in us, but we are unable to make use of it. So we have to give it to the plants, as the 'gas of life'. The plants build up their bodies from this same carbon. The plants can do what the human beings of today cannot do; but which the future human being will be able to achieve.

Visualize this process to yourself. Absorption of the carbon dioxide by the plants: they release oxygen which is then put inside the human being [...*gap in the lecture notes*...] so we shall have, in the future, the coming together of ourselves with the plant world which is taken up into human nature, then we build up, as the plants do today, a pure chaste body (*as the plant body is pure and chaste, including in regard to its reproductive section*). When the human being is on the pathway to working towards this goal consciously, then the human being is also at that higher soul-state which is capable of developing the Chalice of the Holy Grail.

The breathing process is not at all a finalized, closed-off process; it is on the way to becoming ever more perfected, and also capable of bringing about, within the human being, that process which normally occurs outside of the human being; and thereby to metamorphose that human substance which today is permeated by Kama, into pure, chaste substance. This is real alchemy. For the human being will be then of such a state of spirituality that people will have learnt how to transform the cosmos.....the 'Philosopher's Stone' is the coal, it is the substance from which the human body of the future shall be constructed. Naturally the more specific, intimate details (*about this transmuting)* are only given directly by the Teacher to the student.

---

[73] See the book, "*The Vidar Flame Column - its meaning from Rudolf Steiner", for more insights into why the* Holy Grail is regarded with a deep reverence by students of anthroposophy.

COMMENTARY: SEAL SEVEN

From 21st May 1907

Violet spirals (*of the serpents*) (p. 81)
The spiral formations which mainly encompass the tails of the serpents, are painted in a violet colour, but they also have many small mottled areas of a fiery pinkish colour. These pinkish areas point to the beginning of a transformation towards spirituality, in the earthly ego. The violet colour is described by Rudolf Steiner as "somewhat violet", so it is not necessarily a pure violet.

The serpents signify the developing upwards (p. 81)
The snake or serpent has a significant role in many modes of ancient wisdom; in fact, a kind of reverence for serpents existed in ancient times in many cultures. And the serpent as a symbol for various esoteric concepts was very widespread. Two quotes from Rudolf Steiner are useful here:

> "The serpent was viewed in ancient Mystery wisdom as a symbol for development of the spiritual life occurring for a person going through the experience of the material world (*in a spiritually oriented way*). The snake represents what makes possible the destruction of the last manifestation of matter (*in the soul's consciousness*)." [74]

In commenting on the esoteric fairy tale of *The Green Snake and the Beautiful Lily*, by Goethe, Rudolf Steiner explained that the green snake represented the earthly ego which was beginning to seek spirituality, through a humble encountering of life experiences:

> "The green snake symbolises the selfless life-experience – developed in love of wisdom, through experiential wisdom. The snake surrenders its existence, to build a bridge between the sensuality and spirituality."[75]

by purely spiritual cognizing (p. 82)
These are crucial words, emphasizing that the path to initiation is through developing higher consciousness or clairvoyance, in the deeper sense. Here Rudolf Steiner is using 'Erkenntnis' in its highest form ("pure cognizing" - der reinen Erkenntnis) as used by Spinoza). Rudolf Steiner, in his *Goethe's Scientific Worldview* (GA 1, p.78), refers to Spinoza's three levels of Erkenntnis. The highest is "sciential intuitiva" which Rudolf Steiner translates as "anschauende Wissen" that is, 'intuitively-spiritually perceptive knowing' which is, in effect, spiritual cognizing. So here in his lecture on the seal, this word does not mean 'higher knowledge' as such, but spiritual cognizing or initiatory consciousness (from which a direct knowing of spiritual realms develops in oneself). [76] Insight into this challenge, and the help given by the Christ-event for this, glimmers through the ancient writings of the early Christian sage, Clement of Alexandria, when he wrote that, through the Resurrection, and the consequent ascent of Jesus into Heaven (Devachan), "*spiritual perceiving* was bestowed upon us" [77]

The plant chalice is today chaste (p. 82)
Plants have a cup-like or chalice-like structure, known as the calyx, which is formed from its many 'sepals' or outer protective leaf-like parts. So the calyx could be thought

---

[74] Archive Lecture, 29.3.1902.

[75] Rudolf Steiner, *Goethes Geistesart*, p.77 „Die Schlange, die selbstlose, in Liebe zur Weisheit, in erlebter Weisheit entwickelte Lebenserfahrung, gibt ihre Existenz auf, um eine Brücke zu bilden zwischen der Sinnlichkeit und der Geistigkeit."

[76] Hence not by "pure knowledge", as in *Rosicrucianism Renewed* p. 80.

[77] Clement's Greek, about AD 220: to noætôs blepein hæmin dedôrætai: τό νοητῶς βλέπειν ήμιν δεδῶρηται (Miscellanies Bk.1:24)

of as receptacle or chalice. The Latin word 'calyx' is related to the word 'calix' which means a goblet or cup, and from this word we have the term, 'chalice'. It appears that here Rudolf Steiner is asserting that the calyx can be viewed as a type of chalice.

The human being who has become chaste and innocent, is represented by the Dove. (p. 82)
As is well known, the Holy Spirit is symbolized by the dove, and consequently, the sanctified human being is someone who, in Christian terms, has been blessed by the Holy Spirit. This use of the dove indicates how the Christ-impulse is the actual spiritual power that has been nurturing and guiding the person seeking spirituality. This was the case for millennia in antiquity, for the 'cosmic Christ' has been the central spiritual being for long Ages. This deity, or the intermediary of this great god, has been revered in earlier cultures, under other names, such as Ra and Horus, Ahura Mazdao, and Mithra.

However, in addition, the image of the dove in this seal is discretely alluding to another secret of the Grail Mysteries. As the desires for bodily pleasures are overcome, and the reproductive powers are freed of the influence of fallen spiritual forces, then a sanctified etheric-astral force, which was withdrawn from humanity in the Lemurian epoch, at the 'Fall of Man', is restored, to some extent, upon the now chaste initiate. These untainted energies otherwise have only appeared in the world in the etheric body of the Saviour. Through these energies, Jesus was enabled to carry out his extraordinary healings. These unfallen etheric-astral energies are known to initiates as 'the dove forces'.[78]

The Philosopher's Stone
As we noted with seal 4, the Philosopher's Stone refers to a remarkable vivifying of carbon. This is attained through the effect on the etheric body that results from purifying the astral body. The image of a diamond is not mean to imply that the less dense physical body of the future takes on the extreme hardness of a diamond. It is only meant to imply firstly, that this future body will be as pure, or free of dense flesh substances, as is a diamond, and secondly that it shall consist of carbon, but in a transparent, ethereal state.

From 16th Sept 1907

Omitted reference to **Copernicus** (p.83)
The official text has here,

> "You can get an idea of this significance from the following example. Modern astronomy bases its perspective on two sentences from Copernicus...who said that the Sun **also** moves (*not just the Earth and the Moon*). Astronomy has left out a third postulate of his because it is not considered relevant. The Sun is indeed in movement, and in fact, it moves in a spiral motion; and thus the Earth, with the Sun, moves in a complicated, curved trajectory. The same complex motion also involves the Moon, which moves around the Earth. These movements are much more complex that one assumes in basic astronomy."

This paragraph is severely corrupted, resulting in illogical assertions; this is partly due to the omission of several sentences, and partly to the complexity of what was being explained. Rudolf Steiner is indicating briefly here that the motions of the planets

[78] GA 129, lect. 26.August 1911.

around the sun are complex, because the sun itself **is in motion**. He is thereby hinting that these wonderful 'lemniscatory' motions, from the sun's motion, are not just a spatial phenomena, but are also affect the soul; are imprinted into the ennobled aura of the initiate - a viewpoint in harmony with the Ptolemaic solar system. In contradiction to the above official sentence, Copernicus, 1473-1543, writing around 1520, asserted that the sun is motionless. (Also he did not have three postulates, but seven.) It was not until three hundred years later that Sir William Herschel (1738-1822) first began to advance the idea that the sun itself is in motion. So the above official version of this text is meaningless.

What was no doubt said by Rudolf Steiner is that one of those three postulates of the seven stated by Copernicus, which are more specifically related to the Earth's motions, is of little interest to modern astronomy; namely that one which involves the "precession of the equinox". This phrase refers to the apparent motion of the Sun around the zodiac, as seen from the Earth, which causes the 2,160 year zodiacal Ages. This has only a minor relevance to the theme of the serpentine spirals, but it is helpful in indicating that such complex celestial motions do impact on the human soul.

Rudolf Steiner's main point here is complex in itself. He is interweaving Copernican and Ptolemaic views of the solar system. He is specifically saying that, in **contradiction** to Copernicus, the sun is **not stationary** but **does move** in the galaxy; but in **harmony** with Copernicus, he is affirming that the planets **are moving** around the sun, not the Earth. Thus creating their complex curved trajectories as they follow the sun. (He is also affirming the Copernican understanding of the precession of the Equinox.)

Claudius Ptolemy presented the perspective that the Earth is in the centre of the universe, and that the sun, moon and planets are experienced as if moving around our planet. This is an entirely valid viewpoint from the perspective of Earth-dwellers, and of astrology (i.e., spiritual psychology) and of our journey after death. As the planets go around our planet, their energies influence our soul. The implications of what Rudolf Steiner is saying here is that, in harmony with Ptolemy (2nd century AD), but not Copernicus, this motion of the planets around the sun which itself is moving in space, do resonate within the initiated soul on the Earth, and will cause astral-etheric energy patterns in his or her aura. These patterns are different, but caused by the solar lemniscatory motions. It is these wonderfully alive, swirling energy-waves in space and in the aura, which are alluded to in the seventh seal. These are derived from the (anti-Copernican) spatial motion of the sun, and the (pro-Copernican) fact of planets orbiting the sun, which have an impact in the soul, in accordance with the ancient pro-Ptolemaic view of the solar system.

Celestial bodies: a form with which the human shall identify in the future (p. 83)
Behind these veiled words we can glimpse, from what is said above, that the swirling, lemniscatory dancing of the seven classical planets are a living, mobile form of complex energies, which the human soul shall experience and resonate with, in some unspecified sense, in the future.

The reproductive power (*of the human being*) becomes an extract of the Cosmic Power, of the great (*creative*) Cosmic Essence (p. 84)
Very much is implied in this brief sentence. It is indicating that when a high state of purity and wisdom has been attained by the human being, it becomes possible to create a new living being, or to ray forth a powerful energy, by becoming imbued with creative power from the planetary spheres and from the zodiac. But this also means that the human spirit has become by then, a 'co-creator with the gods', having gained the right to be empowered by the divine beings who brought forth Creation.

Every human being, when gazing back into its remote past, sees how he or she went through that process (*born out of the primal Powers of the cosmos*) in the beginning of time. The human being of today also goes through this process, when he or she is born anew out of his or her own (*higher*) powers of consciousness. (p. 84)
Firstly, it appears that this sentence is saying that both the normal human being, after death, and also the initiate of olden times, can survey the origin of the human life-wave. Secondly, that the spiritual seeker in the modern age can also behold this extraordinary panorama, when a high level of clairvoyance has been attained. We could view such a process as being 'born again'.

This sensory death (p. 84)
The phrase appears here in the text without an explanation, but one can conclude that it refers to the cube with the serpents permeating it. That is, the cube has at least two meanings: the future 'diamond body', and secondly, the abstract, earthly thinking, born of existence in the material, physical world. In this sentence it is this second, lower meaning which is meant; the consciousness that 'fallen' humanity has in the physical world, in terms of sense-bound 'dead' thinking or 'deadened consciousness' in general. We can regret that more was not said, or written down, about this last point: "the Secret of the Redeemer". But the person seeking self-initiation on this deep esoteric Rosicrucian-anthroposophical path can meditate upon this phrase.

Overcoming this sensory death in the Primal Fountain of All that is Living (p.84)
With regard to the phrase, 'sensory death' we can now consider some significant revelations from Rudolf Steiner, concerning the inner dynamics of our evolutionary path. We noted earlier that, in terms of zodiacal influences, this Earth Aeon is subject to Taurus; this zodiacal power brings about the densification or solidifying of our world. This Taurean influence was especially powerful in the second half of the Lemurian Epoch. The Earth became ever more dense; mineral substances then appeared for the first time. We could consider the possibility that in the course of human evolution these denser materials, these various minerals, including calcium, need not have permeated the, still soft, fluidic human body. But it was precisely this permeation of the human body by denser matter which higher Powers intended humanity to experience. For only by immersion in a dense material body, and exposed to sensory perceiving, could the sense of a personal "I" arise.

But it was directly through the Taurean influences that human consciousness began to become oriented in this way to the physical realm; as a result, mental images derived from what the senses registered, were experienced. From this process, human consciousness became ever more earth-oriented; and repeated lifetimes in mortal flesh bodies began. And from this, the experience of death entered into humanity's existence.

Rudolf Steiner reports that it is precisely the process of experiencing earthly mental images and ideas, which caused the resonance of the cosmic Word, pulsing through the planet's ethers, to become increasingly deadened within the human being. It is this resonance, this pulsing of cosmic ether energies, from the zodiac and the planets, long ago, through the still soft, ethereal Earth, which are to be seen reflected in the beautiful patterns preserved in gems and rocks. These patterns preserve the 'cosmic dance' of the Earth's minerals when the planet was still soft; these swirling dance motions were caught and frozen in solid matter, as the Earth hardened.
It is a direct result of this deadening of the cosmic resonance in the human being, that mental images (or 'ideation') and associated concepts, related to the dense physical world, filled human consciousness. Rudolf Steiner explains that our normal earthly

thinking is basically a process of forming mental images, that is, a consciousness which cognizes and validates only the material, physical realm

But crucially, he informed an audience in 1908 that it was this very process, of the soul forming earthly mental images and ideas derived from the physical environment, which caused the deadened ash-like mineral substances, appearing in the environment of the hardening planet, **to permeate the soft, malleable human body**. Through this research, Rudolf Steiner has revealed the essential dynamic behind the mystery of how we became earthly beings. This same process - the descent of humans into physical-material bodies - is described in the Book of Genesis as Adam and Eve becoming clothed in "coats of skin" (Gen. 3:21).

In Rudolf Steiner's words,

> "The earthly conceptual thinking process impelled the 'ash' or mineral substances into the living, soft, malleable body; and to the extent that this occurred, to that degree, the calcification process occurred, forming the skeleton. And as this happened, the human being's soul became ever more permeated by self-awareness, by earthly thinking."[79]

It was these processes which over millions of years, created the earthly sense of "I". And it this same process which now needs to be reversed, in a wholesome sense. That is, the sense of self or "I" must be retained, but gradually become ennobled and then extended into functioning on spiritual levels of consciousness. The way to rise above this earthly consciousness is through meditation, wherein the 'cosmic Word', or the revelations of the spiritual world, can once again be experienced by the soul, and thereby ennoble the astral body, and also enliven the etheric body and, in a subtle way, protect the physical body against 'hardening' or coarsening influences.

This quest to develop the Spiritual-self, is that inner need of the human soul which was the reason for the decision made by the cosmic Christ to become incarnate, that is to 'over-shadow' Jesus, and then to unite with the Earth-soul at the Resurrection event, in the sacrifice on Golgotha hill.

For, as the Spiritual-self arises into being, the fountain of its holy radiance is this same cosmic Christ. But for this to occur, the assistance of the human vessel of the Christ, Jesus, the Messiah, is needed; through him, this spiritual 'substance' is offered to the human being. Rudolf Steiner's lecture cycles on the Gospels and his primary text, *An Outline of Esoteric Science* are essential reading to acquire an understanding of the profound esoteric truths behind Christianity. This deepened understanding allows the soul to approach the spiritual temple of the Holy Grail, from which a wonderful light rays forth, guiding the inner life of the soul. From this light, the pathway becomes illumined which leads to developing in oneself the Son of Man.

What have we experienced in our contemplation of the seven seals ? We have seen that, in Ages past, seven remarkable images were formed in the astral realm by spiritual beings; these images are visible to those people who are seers. If the seer is also an initiate, then profoundly valuable insights can be made available by that initiate to students of spiritual wisdom. In a semi-confidential session held during the 1907 Munich Conference, Rudolf Steiner revealed the meaning of the seven 'apocalyptic

---

[79] GA 102 lect. 16. March 1908.

seals'. These images depict dynamics closely related to some scenes portrayed in the Book of Revelation.

Although the transcript of his words at the Conference are defective in many places, we have worked our way through these notes, as well as the transcript of a similar lecture given in September of that year to Theosophists in Stuttgart. It has become clear that these seven images are an invaluable guide to aligning our own will to the will of the gods, regarding the potential in the future for humanity to spiritualize. The first seal depicts the future, perfected human being, "The Son of Man"'; a person who has achieved the Spiritual-self. The next few seals then take us back to the formation of the human being in remote aeons; our astral nature becoming interwoven in the earthly world with that of the animal Group-souls.

The seals then move on into the future, pointing to the series of seven evolutionary periods through which humanity has to travel, on its great but challenging journey towards realizing the presence of the Logos in the Higher-self. We also had to acknowledge the existence of a seven-fold Double or Lower-self in the soul. But we are shown that this can be overcome with the help of the Archangel Michael, and above all, of the Christ. This presence of the Christ-light in the Spiritual-self is portrayed in a deeply esoteric manner, in the seal of the Holy Grail.

By contemplating these seven images, we are in truth 'filling the air around the Earth with spiritual thought-forms' – uplifting and illumining the planet's aura, and aligning our hopes and intentions for the future with the dynamics underlying the future evolutionary cycle of the Earth.

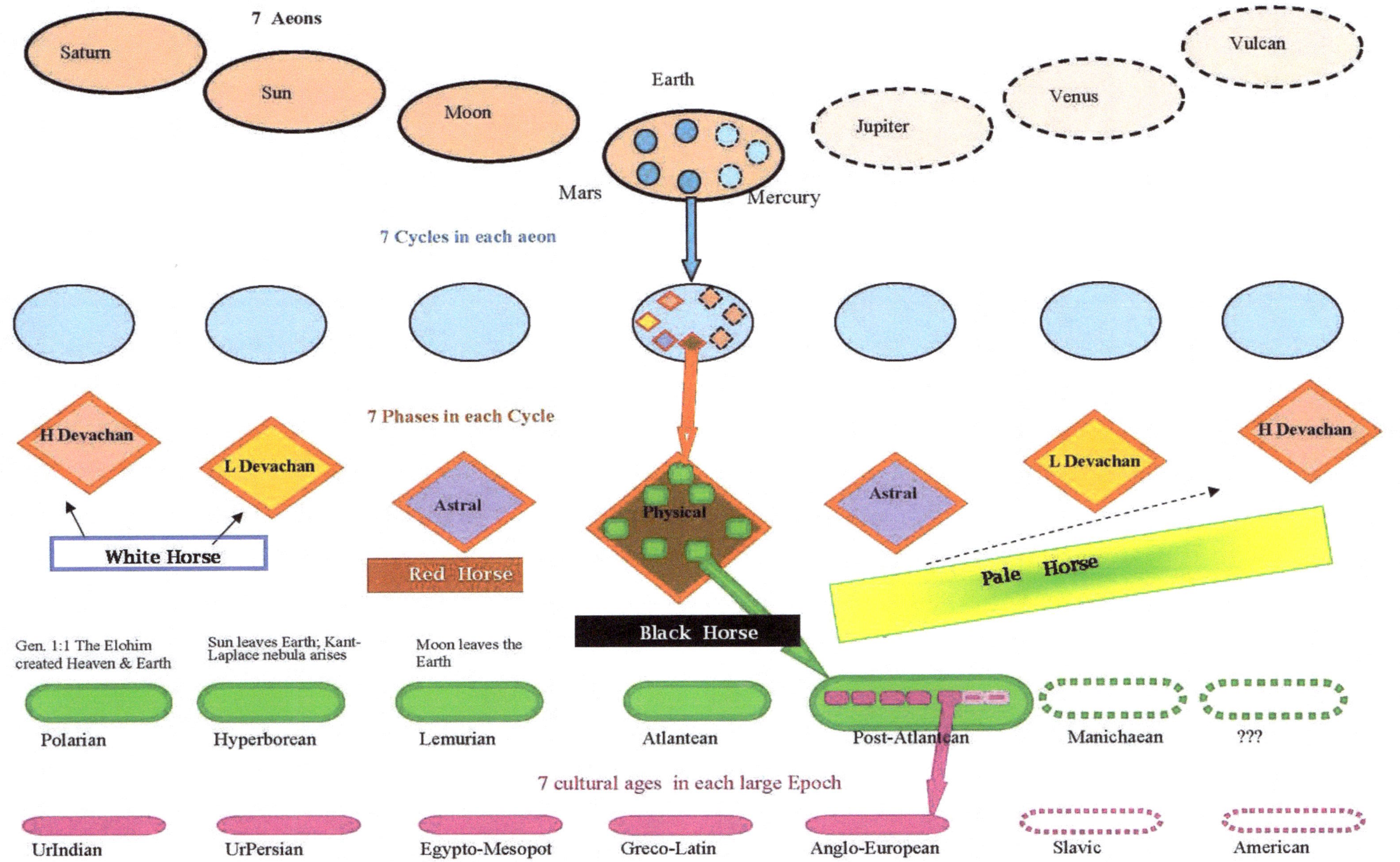

The 4 horsemen in regard to the Phases of the 4th Cycle of our Aeon

Saturday, May 18th.

Morning.

10 o'clock: Opening of the Congress.

1. Musical introduction: F-dur toccata by J. S. Bach. Emanuel Nowotny.
2. Greeting and introductive adress by the General Secretary of the German Section: Dr. Rudolf Steiner (as acting President of the congress).
3. Adresses of General Secretaries of the federated Sections.
4. Adress of Mrs. Besant.

Afternoon.

Beginning: 3 o'çlock.

1. Astrology and Personal Fate. By Alan Leo.
2. Unity and hierarchy. By Dr. Th. Pascal.
3. Lecture of Michael Bauer.
4. The Value of the Theosophical Society. By James Wedgwood.

Evening.

Beginning: 8 o'clock.

1. Preludium and Fugue in h-moll by J. S. Bach. Emanuel Nowotny.
2. Recitation from Goethes Faust, II. part. Marie v. Sivers.
3. Pictures from the East by R. Schumann. Alice v. Sonklar and Toni Völker.
4. Two songs by Fr. Schubert. Gertrude Garmatter.
   a) To music.
   b) Thon art peace.
5. Pastoral and Capriccio by Scarlatti. Toni Völker.

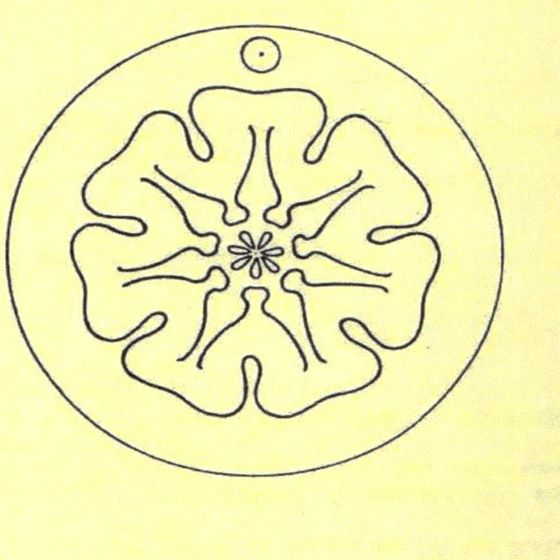

Appendix 2: These substantial artistic contributions were a radical change to the usual arrangements for Theosophical Society conferences.

Sonntag, 19. Mai.

Vormittag.

10 Uhr: Beginn.

1. Trio in Es-dur von Joh. Brahms (1. Satz). Durch Johanna Fritsch, Marika v. Gumppenberg, Hermann Tuckermann.
2. A vision of Hades. By G. R. S. Mead.
3. Theosophie in Russland. Von Anna Kamensky.
4. Die Einweihung des Rosenkreuzers. Von Dr. Rudolf Steiner.

Nachmittag.

5 Uhr: Beginn.

Das heilige Drama von Eleusis. (Aus dem Französischen). Mysterium von Eduard Schuré. Musik von Bernhard Stavenhagen.

Nachher: Geselliges Zusammensein. Ein Buffet ist aufgestellt während der Zwischenakte des Dramas und während des geselligen Zusammenseins.

Sunday, May 19th.

Morning.

Beginning: 10 o'clock.

1. Trio in Es-dur by J. Brahms (1. composition). J. Fritsch, M. v. Gumppenberg, H. Tuckermann.
2. A vision of Hades. By G. R. S. Mead.
3. Theosophy in Russia. By Anna Kamensky.
4. The Initiation of the Rosicrucian. By Dr. Rudolf Steiner.

Afternoon.

Beginning: 5 o'clock.

The Sacred Drama of Eleusis. (Translated from the french.) A Mystery-play by Edouard Schuré. Music by Bernhard Stavenhagen.

Afterwards Social meeting.

A Buffet will be opened during the intervals of the drama and during the social meeting.

Monday, May 20th.

Morning.

Beginning: 10 o'clock.

1. Recitation. By Richard Jürgas.
2. a) Prayer. b) Retirement. c) The sleeping child Jesus. By Hugo Wolf. Elisabeth Lauser.
3. Lecture of Mrs. Besant.
4. Absolute and relative truths. By Arvid Knös.
5. The means for theosophical World-conception. By Dr. Carl Unger.
6. The occult basis of the myth of Siegfried. By Elise Wolfram.

Afternoon.

Beginning: 3½ o'clock.

1. Lecture of Mr. Bailly.
2. Planetary and Human Evolution. By Dr. Rudolf Steiner.

Evening.

Beginning: 8 o'clock.

1. Sonata in g-moll. By L. van Beethoven. (Adagio, Allegro, Rondo). Chr. Döbereiner (violoncell) and Elfriede Schunk (piano).
2. Two songs. Gertrude Garmatter.
   a) Song of Weyla. By Hugo Wolf.
   b) Belief in Spring. By Fr. Schubert.
3. Soli for Viola da Gamba with piano. Chr. Döbereiner and Elfride Schunk.
   a) Adagio. By G. Fr. Händel.
   b) Aria con variazione. By A. Kühnel (composed in 1645).

(The Viola da Gamba [generally used from the end of the 15th century till the end of the 18th century] is strung with six or seven strings in the tune (A), D, G, c, e, a, d̄. In the middle of the 18th century it was removed by the four-stringed violoncell sounding fuller.)

Between 1., 2., 3. members are kindly invited for tea.

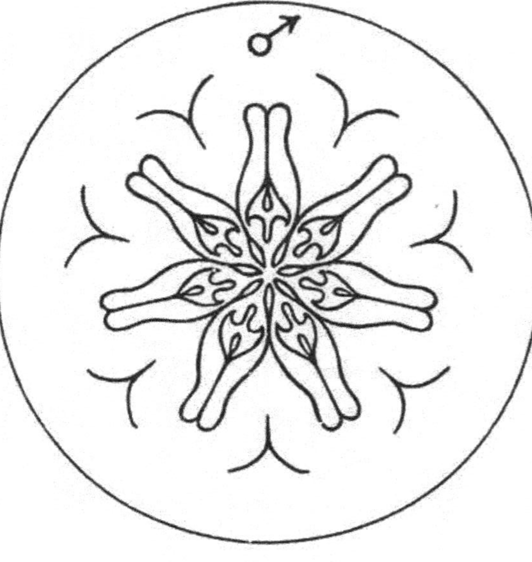

Tuesday, Mai 21th.

Morning.

Beginning: 10 o'clock.

1. Adagio from the Violin Concert, op. 26, by Max Bruch. Johanna Fritsch and Pauline Friess.
2. Recitation by Richard Jürgas and * * *
3. Free Intercourse on theosophical subjects.
   Subjects: a) Necessity of supporting Occultism within the Society.
   b) Questions about education.

Afternoon.

Beginning: 4 o'clock.

In a smaller circle (yet open to every one) conferences will be held about:
Notions about numbers, conception of infiniteness etc.
Above and below „Good and bad".
(Will be continued, if desired, the next day.)

Evening.

Beginning: 9 o'clock. Closing of the Congress.

1. Adagio in D-dur by Adolf Arenson. Adolf Arenson (piano). Johanna Fritsch (violin), Dr. Carl Unger (violoncell).
2. a) Consolation by Felix Mendelssohn-Bartholdy. Hilde Stockmeyer.
   b) Girls song, Tercett by M. Jacobi. Elisabeth Lauser (Soprano), Hilde Stockmeyer (2. Soprano), Gertrude Garmatter (contralto).
   c) Ave Verum by W. A. Mozart. Gertrude Garmatter. Accompaniment on the organ: Emanuel Nowotny.
3. Soli for violin by J. S. Bach. Johanna Fritsch and Pauline Friess.
   a) Air.
   b) Gavotte.
4. Variations about the Choral-Song: Be greeted, kind Jesus. For the organ by J. S. Bach. Emanuel Nowotny.
5. Closing Adresses.

Von Mitgliedern der Gesellschaft ist ein vornehmes vegetarisches Restaurant eben eröffnet worden. Dasselbe befindet sich = Schraudolphstr. 2a (dicht bei der neuen Pinakothek). Die Mitglieder werden dort jederzeit Gelegenheit finden, ihre Mahlzeiten zu ihrer Befriedigung einzunehmen. (Ausser den übrigen Localitäten ist ein separates Theezimmer vorhanden). ~~Von dort~~ Die Leitung dieses Restaurants besorgt auch das Buffet des Congresses.

For this day there is no notice of a lecture by Rudolf Steiner on the Seals; but it was given in the afternoon informal session. (A notice in his hand-writing says that a good vegetarian restaurant is located nearby: this is to be added for the final version.)

APPENDIX 3

From Rudolf Steiner: two meditations on the Spiritual Sun

Unveil, O Infinite One, Thy countenance.
Thou whom dost nurture the universe.
From whom all things derive and to whom all things return.
Remove from our eyes the veil of delusion,
Reveal Thyself to us, O Sun of wisdom!
Thou whom art hidden in the shimmer of Thy golden light,
That we on the mighty path of the Ancient Wisdom
May perceive the Truth in the humble, living teachings of Christ
And thereby fulfil the purpose of our existence.
May Thou teach me that I can perceive the depths of existence.
May Thou instruct me that I can fulfil in truth my duties.
May Thou illumine me that I may behold my oneness in Thee,
For this alone leads to perception of God,
And to eternal peace.
Amen.

(This meditative prayer was also given in a second version, as follows: it is possible that the former one is to be meditated on in the morning, and the latter in the evening.)

Thou whom dost illumine the universe,
May Thou illumine me also, and remove
The veil from my eyes, that I may behold the true Sun.
For it is still hidden from me;
Yet its shimmering radiance gleams through my soul,
Like a sea of golden light.
O grant that I may see it in full clarity, the pure truth.
Grant that in its light I may recognize what my life duties are,
And when my journey has ended, allow me to reach its holy place.
O Thou comforter of all creation, give me the strength
to truly attain unto this place, the realm of the spiritual Sun.
O thou who art Love Divine, receive me into Thy purpose
And keep pure in me the eternal rays of faithful will.
Amen.

Index

GLOSSARY of some central anthroposophical terms

Aeon: a long evolutionary time. There are seven of these, and we are now in the fourth such epoch. They are the Saturn, Sun, Moon, Earth (which has two halves, Mars and Mercury) Jupiter, Venus and Vulcan aeons.

Ahriman: an evil entity responsible for the attitude which sees matter as the only thing in creation, denying spiritual reality. It correlates to the Biblical term, Satan.

Angels: spiritual beings who are one aeon ahead of human beings in their evolution.

anthroposophy: a Greek word that literally means 'human-soul wisdom'. In Rudolf Steiner's usage it means the wisdom that can dawn in a person's consciousness, in their spiritual-soul; and which fully manifests when the Spiritual-self is developed.

Archangels: spiritual beings who are two aeons ahead of human beings in their evolution.

astral body: the soul, seen as an aura around the body.

astral realm: the Soul-world, above the ethers, but below the Devachanic realms.

astrality: soul energies, but often it refers mainly to the feelings.

Buddhi Plane: a divine realm more transcendent than Devachan; where the Bodhisattvas exist

Consciousness-soul: (see spiritual-soul)

Cosmic Christ: the highest of the 'Powers' or sun-gods.

Devachan: the true heavens above the Soul-world; a Theosophical term from the Sanskrit meaning 'realm of the shining gods'; it is the realm of the archetypal Idea of Plato.

the Double: a term usually referring to the Lower Self.

ego or self or I: the sense of self, but the eternal self is linked to this. Hence the ego is a dual or twofold thing.

egoism or egoistic: not quite the same as the well-known term egotism (which means conceit). Egoism is used by Rudolf Steiner to mean either the state of having a normal earth-centred ego, or for this earthly sense of self behaving in a selfish way.

etheric body: is made of the four ethers and duplicates the physical body's appearance, from which organic matter, such as new cells, are condensed.

ethers: subtle energies which sustain all living things on the Earth. Electricity and magnetism are formed as the ethers decompose.

Group-soul: a spirit-being to whom all the animals of a particular species belong.

intellectual-soul: the rational, logical capacity.

Imagination, Inspiration, Intuition: Latin words for the three types of clairvoyance, but which mean something different in everyday usage in English to the meanings that Rudolf Steiner gives them.

Imagination: the first stage of clairvoyance; can be called 'psychic-image consciousness'. It brings perception of astral or etheric images, (usually means 'fantasy'.)

Imaginations: astral thought-forms.

Inspiration: this can be called 'cosmic-spiritual consciousness', it is a perceiving or 'breathing-in' wisdom, from lower Devachan. (In normal English usually this word means a strongly felt creative urge or idea.)

Intuition: this can be called a 'High initiation consciousness'. It is a perceiving of another being by inwardly becoming one with that being. This state allows the seer to perceive at an upper Devachan level. (In normal English this word usually means a semi-psychic awareness of something.)

intuition: can be used by Rudolf Steiner for the above high seership, but it can sometimes appear in English anthroposophical texts in its usual English meaning of 'insights' (translating such German words as 'ahnen').

life-force: an alternative term for ether.

life-force organism: the ether body.

Life-spirit: the divinized etheric body, is made of Devachanic energies.

lower-self: the soul qualities that are tainted with Luciferic or Ahrimanic influences. It can be thought of as threefold, the lower thinking, feeling and will. But Rudolf Steiner also described it as sevenfold, being the lower qualities of the seven classical planets in astrology.

Lucifer: a 'fallen' entity who opposes the intentions of the higher gods, creating an ungrounded, naïve attitude in human beings, but also instils a sense of self and enthusiasm for beauty, art and sensuality.

sentient-soul: the feelings, the emotion capacities of the soul.

soul: appears as an aura, and contains the sentient-soul, intellectual-soul and spiritual-soul.

Spirit-human: the divine forces underlying the physical body, in our subconscious will.

Spiritual-self: the result of the purified and enlightened threefold soul-body or astral body.

spiritual-soul: also translated as ‘consciousness soul’, and could be called the intuitive soul. This is the soul capacity which underlies intuitive decision-making or intuitive flashes of insight. But it is also the most individualized or ‘ego-ic’ soul capacity, and can tend towards a hardened self-centredness.

Spiritual-sun: the sun on its soul (or astral) level, behind the physical globe, and also on its actual spiritual level (also referred to as the Devachanic level): these levels comprise many energies and divine beings.

thinking: can be used to mean the exercise of our intelligence, but it is also used to mean any of the three clairvoyant states we can attain.

Books by this Author

Living a Spiritual Year: seasonal festivals in both hemispheres (new, expanded edition, 2016)	1992
The Way to the Sacred	2003
The Foundation Stone Meditation: a new commentary	2005
Dramatic Anthroposophy: Identification and contextualization of primary features of Rudolf Steiner's anthroposophy. (PhD thesis)	2005
Two Gems from Rudolf Steiner	2014
The Hellenistic Mysteries & Christianity	2014
Rudolf Steiner Handbook	2014
Horoscope Handbook – a Rudolf Steiner Approach	2015
The Meaning of the Goetheanum Windows	2016
The Lost Zodiac of Rudolf Steiner	2016
Rudolf Steiner's Esoteric Christianity in the Grail painting by Anna May	2017
The Vidar Flame Column – its meaning from Rudolf Steiner	2017
Rudolf Steiner on Leonardo's *Last Supper*	2017
Blessed - Rudolf Steiner on the Beatitudes	2018
Rudolf Steiner's First Class Verses	2019
The Soul's Calendar - annotated with Commentary	2020
The Soul's Calendar - pocket edition	2020
The Apocalyptic Seals from Rudolf Steiner	2020

Also, under the pen-name Damien Pryor:

The nature & origin of the Tropical Zodiac	2011
Stonehenge	2011
Lalibela	2011
The Externsteine	2011
The Great Pyramid & the Sphinx	2011

Website: www.rudolfsteinerstudies.com

This site has information on all of these books, as well as free downloads of various essays, and a link to the author's ARTPRINTS page, which offers esoteric diagrams and great classical works of art which are relevant to the understanding of anthroposophy.

www.ingramcontent.com/pod-product-compliance
Lightning Source LLC
LaVergne TN
LVHW060615110826
845154LV00003B/94

9780648135883